DOING YOUR RESEARCH PROJECT

DOING YOUR RESEARCH PROJECT

A GUIDE FOR FIRST-TIME RESEARCHERS IN EDUCATION AND SOCIAL SCIENCE

Judith Bell

Open University Press
Milton Keynes · Philadelphia

Open University Press
Celtic Court
22 Ballmoor
Buckingham MK18 1XW
and
1900 Frost Road, Suite 101
Bristol, PA 19007, USA

First Published 1987
Reprinted 1988, 1989 (twice), 1991

British Library Cataloguing in Publication Data

Bell, Judith, *1930-*
    Doing your research project: a guide for first-time
    researchers in education and social science.
    1. Education — Research
    I. Title
    370'.72   LB1028

ISBN 0-335-15988-5
ISBN 0-335-15987-7 Pbk

Library of Congress in Cataloging No. 86–28431

Text design by Carlton Hill
Typeset by Burns & Smith, Derby
Printed in Great Britain by J. W. Arrowsmith Ltd., Bristol

This book is derived in part from course material written for Part B of the Open University Advanced Diploma in Educational Management (EP851). The material has been substantially adapted and new chapters written to extend the scope of the original work. Information about EP851 and the Advanced Diploma in Educational Management may be obtained from any Open University regional centre, from the EP851 course manager or from the Associate Student Central Office at the Open University, Walton Hall, Milton Keynes MK7 6AA.

Contents

Acknowledgements

I have been helped throughout the preparation of this book by the interest of colleagues and friends who were once first-time researchers themselves but are now expert practitioners. I should like particularly to thank Sandy Goulding and Ian McNay, former colleagues at the Open University, who never failed to provide assistance when requested. Sandy wrote Chapter 11 and both saw drafts at various stages. My thanks also to Sally Baker, librarian at the Open University, for assistance with Chapter 3; to Alan Woodley, Research Fellow at the Open University, for permission to reproduce the literature review in Chapter 3; to Dr Michael Youngman, senior lecturer in educational research methods at the University of Nottingham, for permission to quote his seven question types in Chapter 7.

A special word of thanks to Dr Brendan Duffy and Stephen Waters, who, as two of the first Open University EP851 students, carried out investigations into aspects of educational management in their own institutions and developed a considerable degree of expertise in research methods in the process. Stephen allowed me to quote his views on 'inside' research in Chapter 5, on interviews in Chapter 8 and to use an abstract (which he prepared in connection with an EP851 project) in Chapter 12. Brendan wrote Chapter 6 and contributed to Chapters 4 and 12. Both read drafts and provided helpful comments.

To them, to members of the Open University EP851 course team who commented on course materials, some of which are included in this book, and to everyone else who offered advice, pointed out omissions and errors, my grateful thanks.

Judith Bell

Introduction

This book is intended for those of you who are about to undertake some sort of educational research in connection with your job, or as a requirement for an undergraduate, diploma or postgraduate course.

If you are a beginner researcher, the problems facing you are much the same whether you are producing a small project, an MEd dissertation or a PhD thesis. You will need to select a topic, identify the objectives of your study, plan and design a suitable methodology, devise research instruments, negotiate access to institutions, materials and people, collect, analyse and present information and finally, produce a well-written report or dissertation. Whatever the size of the undertaking, techniques have to be mastered and a plan of action devised which does not attempt more than the limitations of expertise, time and access permit. Large-scale research projects will require sophisticated techniques and, often, statistical and computational expertise, but it is quite possible to produce a worthwhile study without using computers and with a minimum of statistical knowledge.

We all learn how to do research by actually doing it, but a great deal of time can be wasted and goodwill dissipated by inadequate preparation. This book aims to provide you with the tools to do the job, to help you to avoid some of the pitfalls and time-wasting false trails that can eat into your time allowance, to establish good research habits and to take you from the stage of selecting a topic through to the production of a well-planned, methodologically sound and well-written final report or dissertation—ON TIME. There is, after all, little point in doing all the work if you never manage to submit.

Throughout this book, I use the terms 'research', 'investigation', 'inquiry' and 'study' interchangeably, though I realize this is not acceptable to everyone.

Some argue that 'research' is a more rigorous and technically more complicated form of investigation. Howard and Sharp discuss this issue in *The Management of a Student Research Project:*

> Most people associate the word 'research' with activities which are substantially removed from day-to-day life and which are pursued by outstandingly gifted persons with an unusual level of commitment. There is of course a good deal of truth in this viewpoint, but we would argue that the pursuit is not restricted to this type of person and indeed can prove to be a stimulating and satisfying experience for many people with a trained and enquiring mind.

> (Howard and Sharp 1983:6)

They define research (p.6) as 'seeking through methodical processes to add to one's own body of knowledge and, hopefully, to that of others, by the discovery of non-trivial facts and insights'.

Drew (1980) agrees that 'research is conducted to solve problems and to expand knowledge' (p.4) and stresses that 'research is a systematic way of asking questions, a systematic method of enquiry' (p.8). It is the *systematic* approach that is important in the conduct of your projects, not the title of 'research', 'investigation', 'inquiry' or 'study'. Where collection of data is involved (notes of interviews, questionnaire responses, articles, official reports, minutes of meetings, etc.), orderly record-keeping and thorough planning are essential.

No book can take the place of a good supervisor, but good supervisors are in great demand, and if you can familiarize yourself with basic approaches and techniques, you will be able to make full use of your tutorial time for priority issues.

The examples given in the following chapters relate particularly to projects which have to be completed in two to three months (what I have called the '100-hour' projects), but I hope the material will be equally useful for those of you who are about to undertake research leading to a higher degree.

Part I

PREPARING THE GROUND

1

Approaches to Educational Research

It is perfectly possible to carry out a worthwhile investigation without having detailed knowledge of the various approaches to or styles of educational research, but a study of different approaches will give insight into different ways of planning an investigation, and, incidentally, will also enhance your understanding of the literature. One of the problems of reading about research methods and reading research reports is the terminology. Researchers use terms and occasionally jargon that may be incomprehensible to other people. It is the same in any field, where a specialized language develops to ease communication among professionals. So, before considering the various stages of planning and conducting investigations, it may be helpful to consider the main features of certain well-established and well-reported styles of research.

Different styles, traditions or approaches use different methods of collecting data, but no approach prescribes nor automatically rejects any particular method. Quantitative researchers collect facts and study the relationship of one set of facts to another. They measure, using scientific techniques that are likely to produce quantified and, if possible, generalizable conclusions. Researchers adopting a qualitative perspective are more concerned to understand individuals' perceptions of the world. They seek insight rather than statistical analysis. They doubt whether social 'facts' exist and question whether a 'scientific' approach can be used when dealing with human beings. Yet there are occasions when qualitative researchers draw on quantitative techniques, and *vice versa*.

Classifying an approach as quantitative or qualitative, ethnographic, survey, action research or whatever, does not mean that once an approach has been selected, the researcher may not move from the methods normally associated with that style. Each approach has its strengths and weaknesses and each is particularly suitable for a particular context. The approach adopted and the methods of data collection selected will depend on the nature of the inquiry and the type of information required.

It is impossible in the space of a few pages to do justice to any of the well-established styles of research, but the following will at least provide a basis for further reading and may give you ideas about approaches which you may wish to adopt in your own investigation.

Action Research and the 'Teacher as Researcher' Model

There are many definitions of action research. Cohen and Manion describe it as

> essentially an on-the-spot procedure designed to deal with a concrete problem located in an immediate situation. This means that the step-by-step process is constantly monitored (ideally, that is) over varying periods of time and by a variety of mechanisms (questionnaires, diaries, interviews and case studies, for example) so that the ensuing feedback may be translated into modifications, adjustments, directional changes, redefinitions, as necessary, so as to bring about lasting benefit to the ongoing process itself
>
> (Cohen and Manion 1980:178)

As they point out, an important feature of action research is that the task is not finished when the project ends. The participants continue to review, evaluate and improve practice. Brown and McIntyre, who describe an action-research model for curriculum innovation in Scottish schools, also emphasize the on-going nature of the method. They write:

> The research questions arise from an analysis of the problems of the practitioners in the situation and the immediate aim then becomes that of understanding those problems. The researcher/actor, at an early stage, formulates speculative, tentative, general principles in relation to the problems that have been identified; from these principles, hypotheses may then be generated about what action is likely to lead to the desired improvements in practice. Such action will then be tried out and data on its effects collected; these data are used to revise the earlier hypotheses and identify more appropriate action that reflects a modification of the general principles. Collection of data on the effects of this new action may then generate further hypotheses and modified principles, and so on as we move towards a greater understanding and improvement of practice. This implies a continuous process of research and the worth of the work is judged by the understanding of, and desirable change in, the practice that is achieved.
>
> (Brown and McIntyre 1981:245)

The essentially practical, problem-solving nature of action research makes this approach attractive to practitioner-researchers who have identified a problem during the course of their work, see the merit of investigating it and, if possible, of improving practice. There is nothing new about practitioners operating as researchers, and the 'teacher as researcher' model has been extensively discussed (Bartholomew 1971, Cope and Gray 1979, Raven and Parker 1981).

Action research is not, of course, limited to projects carried out by teachers in an educational setting. It is appropriate in any context when 'specific knowledge is required for a specific problem in a specific situation, or when a new approach is to be grafted on to an existing system' (Cohen and Manion 1980:181). Action research needs to be planned in the same systematic way as any other type of research, and the methods selected for gathering information will depend on the nature of the information required. Action research is not a method or technique. It is an approach which has proved to be particularly attractive to educators because of its practical, problem-solving emphasis, because practitioners (sometimes with researchers from outside the institution; other times not) carry out the research and because the research is directed towards greater understanding and improvement of practice *over a period of time*.

Case Study

The case-study approach is particularly appropriate for individual researchers because it gives an opportunity for one aspect of a problem to be studied in some depth within a limited time scale (though some case studies are carried out over a long period of time, as with Elizabeth Richardson's [1973] three-year study of Nailsea School).

Case study has been described as 'an umbrella term for a family of research methods having in common the decision to focus on inquiry around an instance' (Adelman *et al.*, 1977). It is much more than a story about or a description of an event or state. As in all research, evidence is collected systematically, the relationship between variables is studied and the study is methodically planned. Case study is concerned principally with the interaction of factors and events and, as Nisbet and Watt (1980:5) point out, 'sometimes it is only by taking a practical instance that we can obtain a full picture of this interaction'. Though observation and interviews are most frequently used in case study, no method is excluded. Methods of collecting information are selected which are appropriate for the task.

The great strength of the case-study method is that it allows the researcher to concentrate on a specific instance or situation and to identify, or attempt to identify, the various interactive processes at work. These processes may remain hidden in a large-scale survey but may be crucial to the success or failure of systems or organizations.

Case studies may be carried out to follow up and to put flesh on the bones of a survey. They can precede a survey and be used as a means of identifying key issues which merit further investigation, but the majority of case studies are carried out as free-standing exercises. The researcher identifies an 'instance', which could be the introduction of a new syllabus, the way a school adapts to a new role, or any innovation or stage of development in an institution — and observes, questions, studies. Each organization has its common and its unique features. The case-study researcher aims to identify such features and to show how they affect the implementation of systems and influence the way an organization functions.

Inevitably, where a single researcher is gathering all the information, selection has to be made. The researcher selects the area for study and decides which material to present in the final report. It is difficult to cross-check information and so there is always the danger of distortion. Critics of the case-study approach draw attention to this and other problems. They point to the fact that generalization is not usually possible and question the value of the study of single events.

Much educational research does seek to generalize and to contribute to the development of educational theory, but it is unlikely that research of the size we are considering whether case study or not, will achieve such aims. That is not to say that the study of single events is not worth while and supporters of case study make a strong case for this approach.

Bassey takes the view that

> an important criterion for judging the merit of a case study is the extent to which the details are sufficient and appropriate for a teacher working in a similar situation to relate his decision making to that described in the case study. The relatability of a case study is more important than its generalisability
>
> (Bassey 1981:85).

He considers that if case studies

> are carried out systematically and critically, if they are aimed at the improvement of education, if they are relatable, and if by publication of the findings they extend the boundaries of existing knowledge, then they are valid forms of educational research.
>
> (p.86)

A successful study will provide the reader with a three-dimensional picture and will illustrate relationships, micropolitical issues and patterns of influences in a particular context.

The Ethnographic Style

The ethnographic style of fieldwork research was developed originally by anthropologists who wished to study a society or some aspect of a society, culture or group in depth. They developed an approach which depended heavily on observation and, in some cases, complete or partial integration into the society being studied. This form of participant observation enabled the researchers, as far as was possible, to share the same experiences as the subjects and so to understand better why they acted in the way they did. This approach is no longer limited to anthropological studies and has been effectively used in a good many studies of small groups.

Participant observation takes time and so is often outside the scope of researchers working on 100-hour projects. The researcher has to be accepted by the individuals or groups being studied, and this can mean doing the same job or living in the same environment and circumstances as the subjects for lengthy periods. Time is not the only problem with this approach. As in case studies, critics point to the problem of representativeness. If the researcher is studying one group in depth over a period of time, who is to say that group is typical of other groups which may have the same title? Are teachers in one school necessarily representative of teachers in a similar school in another part of the country? Are canteen workers in one type of organization likely to be typical of all canteen workers? Generalizability may be a problem, but as in the case-study approach the study may be relatable in a way that will enable members of similar groups to recognize problems and, possibly, to see ways of solving similar problems in their own group.

Surveys

The aim of a survey is to obtain information which can be analysed and patterns extracted and comparisons made. The census is one example of a survey in which the same questions are asked of the selected population (the population being the group or category of individuals selected). The census aims to cover 100 per cent of the population, but most surveys have less ambitious aims. In most cases, a survey will aim to obtain information from a representative selection of the population and from that sample will then be able to present the findings as being representative of the population as a whole. Inevitably, there are problems in the survey method. Great care has to be taken to ensure that the sample population is truly representative. At a very simple level, that means ensuring that if the total population has 1000 men and 50 women, then the same proportion of men to women has to be selected. But that example grossly oversimplifies the method of drawing a representative sample, and if you decide to carry out a survey, you will need to consider what characteristics of the total population need to be represented in your sample to enable you to say with fair confidence that your sample is reasonably representative.

In surveys, all respondents will be asked the same questions in, as far as possible, the same circumstances. Question wording is not as easy as it seems, and careful piloting is necessary to ensure that all questions mean the same to all respondents. Information can be gathered by means of self-completion questionnaires (as in the case of the census) or by means of questionnaires, schedules or checklists administered by an interviewer. Whichever method of information gathering is selected, the aim is to obtain answers to the same questions from a large number of individuals to enable the researcher not only to describe but also to compare, to relate one characteristic to another and to demonstrate that certain features exist in certain categories. Surveys can provide answers to the questions What? Where? When? and How?, but it is not so easy to find out Why? Causal relationships can rarely if ever be proved by survey method. The main emphasis is on fact-finding, and if a survey is well structured and piloted, it can be a relatively cheap and quick way of obtaining information.

The Experimental Style

It is relatively easy to plan experiments which deal with measurable phenomena. For example, experiments have been set up to measure the effects of using fluoridated toothpaste on dental caries by establishing a control group (who did not use the toothpaste) and an experimental group (who did). In such experiments, the two groups, matched for age, sex, ratio of boys to girls, social class and so on were given a pre-test dental examination and instructions about which toothpaste to use. After a year, both groups were given the post-test dental examination and conclusions were then drawn about the effectiveness or otherwise of the fluoridated toothpaste. The principle of such experiments is that if two identical groups are selected, one of which (the experimental group) is given special treatment and the other (the control group) is not, then any differences between the two groups at the end of the experimental period may be attributed to the difference in treatment. A causal relationship has been established. It may be fairly straightforward to test the extent of dental caries (though even in this experiment the extent of the caries could be caused by many factors not controlled by the experiment), but it is quite another matter to test changes in behaviour. As Wilson (1979) points out, social causes do not work singly. Any examination of low school attainment or high IQ is the product of multiple causes.

> To isolate each cause requires a new experimental group each time and the length and difficulty of the experiment increases rapidly. It is possible to run an experiment in which several treatments are put into practice simultaneously but many groups must be made available rather than just two . . . The causes of social phenomena are usually multiple ones and an experiment to study them requires large numbers of people often for lengthy periods. This requirement limits the usefulness of the experimental method.
>
> (Wilson 1979: 22)

So, the experimental style does allow conclusions to be drawn about cause and effect, if the experimental design is sound, but in education and the social sciences generally, large groups are needed if the many variations and ambiguities involved in human behaviour are to be controlled. Such large-scale experiments are expensive to set up and take more time than most students working on 100-hour projects can give. Some tests which require only a few hours (e.g. to test short-term memory or perception) can be very effective, but in claiming a causal relationship, great care needs to be taken to ensure that all possible causes have been considered.

Which Approach?

Classifying an approach as ethnographic, qualitative, experimental, or whatever, does not mean that once an approach has been selected, the researcher may not move from the methods normally associated with that style. But understanding the major advantages and disadvantages of each approach is likely to help you to select the most appropriate methodology for the task in hand. This chapter covers only the very basic principles associated with the different styles or approaches to research which will suffice — at any rate until you have decided on a topic and considered what information you need to obtain. If you wish to read further, you will find guidance in the reference section at the end of this book.

2

Planning the Project

Selecting a Topic

You may be given a topic to research, in which case the decision is already taken for you, but in most cases you will be asked to select a topic from a list or to decide on a topic yourself. You may have an idea or a particular area of interest that you would like to explore. You may have several ideas, all equally interesting. If so, write them down. *Falling rolls, the role of the head of department of English, something to do with curriculum innovation, staff development.* All good topics, but before a decision is made about which to select, some work needs to be done. You will not have time to read extensively on each topic, but consult the library catalogue to see how much has been written, inquire in the library about dissertations and articles which may have been written on similar topics and talk to your colleagues and fellow students. Talking through problems and possible topics with colleagues is an essential stage of any plan. Their views may differ from or even conflict with your own and may suggest alternate lines of inquiry They may be aware of sensitive aspects of certain topics which could cause difficulties at some stage or know of recent publications which are not listed in the library catalogue. If you are hoping to carry out your research in your own institution, then another very good reason for discussing possible topics with colleagues is that you will probably be asking for their support and collaboration: early consultation is essential if you are to avoid difficulties later.

Selecting a topic is more difficult than it seems at first. With limited time at your disposal there is a temptation to select a topic before the ground work has been done, but try to resist the temptation. Prepare the ground work well and you will save time later. Your discussions and inquiries will help you to select a topic which is likely to be of interest, which you have a good chance of completing, which will be worth the effort and which may even have some practical application later on.

Many educational researchers stress the desirability of considering the practical outcomes of research. Langeveld makes the point that

> Educational studies . . . are a 'practical science' in the sense that we do not only want to know facts and to understand relations for the sake of knowledge, we want to know and understand in order to be able to act and act 'better' than we did before.

> (Langeveld 1965:4)

This is not to deny the importance of educational research that may not have an immediate practical outcome. Eggleston provides a timely reminder of the importance of longer-term objectives and of the need to look beyond current educational practices. To restrict educational research to current educational practices would, in his opinion, lay it 'open to the charge that its sole function was to increase the efficiency of the existing system in terms of accepted criteria and deny it the opportunity to explore potentially more effective alternatives' (Eggleston 1979:5).

Clearly the need for exploring potentially more effective alternatives to the present educational provision will always exist. After 100 hours of study, you are unlikely to be in a position to make recommendations for fundamental change in the educational system. However, whatever the size and scope of the study, you will in all cases analyse and evaluate the information you collect and you may then be in a position to suggest action which will bring about changes in policy and/or improvements in practice.

Discuss possible practical outcomes with your supervisor and decide what the emphasis of your study is to be. Is applicability to be important or is your study to have different aims? Once you have decided on a topic, the precise focus of the study needs to be established. You will need to decide exactly which aspects of your topic are to be investigated and to consider the questions you would like to ask.

The 'First Thoughts' List and Establishing the Focus of the Study

In a short project it is not possible to do everything, so consider your priorities. If you have decided that you are investigating the role of the governing body of your institution, for example, draw up a 'first thoughts' list of questions. At this stage the order and wording are not important. Your aim is to write down all possible questions. You will refine and order them later on. Your list might be on the following lines:

1. What exactly does the governing body of your school/college do?
2. What issues or topics take up most time at governors' meetings?
3. Do governors really have any interest in or influence over the curriculum?
4. How do the head and other staff view the role of the governing body in the running of the institution?
5. What could be done to improve communications between school/college and the governors?
6. How many of the governors would welcome involvement in the curriculum?

7. How often are curriculum issues discussed in governors' meetings?
8. Which aspects of the curriculum are discussed?
9. To what extent do governors feel involved in different areas of the curriculum?
10. Which curricular tasks, if any, have members of the governing body undertaken (e.g. discussing proposed curricular change, evaluating teaching methods, evaluating aims and objectives of the curriculum, etc.).

At this point you may realize that it will be necessary to find out what different categories of governor understand by 'the curriculum' and to investigate the way different individuals perceive their role. You may need to find out whether the teaching staff view the curriculum in the same way as the governors. When you review your list, ask yourself precisely what you mean by each question. If you were to ask governors 'Would you welcome increased involvement in curricular matters?', you would have to specify what you mean by 'curricular matters'. Are *you* clear what you mean? As you subject yourself to rigorous examination of each question, you will begin to clarify what the aims and objectives of your study are and to establish the focus of the study. Each stage is a process of refining and clarifying so that you end with a list of questions, tasks or objectives which you can ask, perform or examine. Decide exactly what it is you are trying to find out and why. Asking why you need certain information will help you to eliminate irrelevant items and will focus your attention on important aspects of the topic.

Hypothesis or Objectives?

Many research projects begin with the statement of a hypothesis, defined by Verma and Beard as

> a tentative proposition which is subject to verification through subsequent investigation. It may also be seen as the guide to the researcher in that it depicts and describes the method to be followed in studying the problem. In many cases hypotheses are hunches that the researcher has about the existence of relationship between variables.
>
> (Verma and Beard 1981:184)

In most experimental and some survey studies a hypothesis is postulated, and the research is structured in such a way as to enable the hypothesis to be tested. Some qualitative studies start without a hypothesis or objectives being specified. The investigators will have an idea about what they are doing, but they do not devise detailed procedures before they begin. The study structures the research rather than the other way round (Bogdan and Biklen 1982:38–44).

There are dangers in this approach, and even experienced researchers occasionally end up with a huge quantity of data and little idea of what to do with it. Collecting everything in sight in the hope that some pattern will emerge is not to be recommended.

Small-scale projects of the kind discussed in this book will not require the statistical testing of hypotheses often required in large-scale sample surveys. Unless your supervisor advises otherwise, a precise statement of objectives is generally quite sufficient. The important point is not so much whether there is a hypothesis, but whether you have carefully thought about what is, and what is not, worth investigating and how the investigation will be conducted. It may be permissible to make minor modifications of objectives as the study proceeds, but that does not obviate the necessity of identifying exactly what you plan to do at the outset. Until that stage has been achieved, it is not possible to consider an appropriate methodology.

The Project Outline

When you are quite clear what the objectives of the study are, draw up an initial project outline to establish a framework within which you can work. The outline will no doubt have to be adapted as the research develops, but a first attempt on the following lines will let you see where you are going.

Provisional title: The Role of the Governing Body
Aim: To investigate the extent to which the governing body plays an active part in oversight of the school's curriculum

Questions to be investigated
1. Is the school accountable for its curriculum to the governing body in any practical sense?
2. How much consultation occurs between the head and the governing body in relation to curricular issues?
3. Are/were the governors involved in determining the aims of the school?
4. To what extent are governors involved in decisions relating to religious education in the school?
5. How many of the governors would welcome increased involvement in curricular matters?
6. How realistic is the concept of partnership between the school, the local education authority (LEA) and the governing body in terms of the curriculum in this school?
7. Do teacher governors suffer role conflict in their relationship to the curriculum?

(Continued)

(Continued)

8. How do teachers view moves towards increased involvement by lay governors?
9. How much training (if any) have governors received?

Possible methods of investigation
1. Documents:
   Articles and instrument of government
   LEA 'Advice to Governors'
   Minutes of meetings
2. Observational analysis: three governors' meetings (spring, summer, autumn).
3. Questionnaire to members of governing body.
4. Interviews with the head, clerk to the governing body, teacher governor, parent governor, governor representing the ancillary staff, pupil governor (may be problematic), co-opted governor, LEA governor, community governor
   [N.B. the questionnaire will form the basis for structured interview schedule]

Literature to be consulted (may be extended later)
Taylor, T. (1977). *Committee of Enquiry into the Management and Government of Schools: 'A New partnership for our Schools'.* Report of the Committee of Enquiry. London, HMSO.
Bacon, W. (1978). *Public Accountability and the Schooling System: A Sociology of School Board Democracy.* London, Harper & Row.
Sallis, J. (1977). *School Managers and Governors: Taylor and After.* London, Ward Lock Educational.
Bennett, N. and Gray, L. (1983) 'Governing Bodies and the Curriculum', in *School Organization* 3(1).
Kogan, M. (ed.) (1984). *School Governing Bodies.* London, Heinemann.

Title

In this working outline, the title is given as 'provisional'. The final version of the title should tell the reader precisely what the study is about, and so you will only be ready to devise a title when you are clear about the focus of the study. 'The role of the governing body' will serve for the time being, but a subtitle might clarify the nature of the topic.

Timing

There is never enough time to do all the work that seems to be essential in order to do a thorough job, but if you have a handover date, then somehow, the work has to be completed in the specified time. It is unlikely that you will be able to keep rigidly to a timetable, but some attempt should be made to devise a schedule so that you can check progress periodically and, if necessary, force yourself to move from one stage of the research to the next.

If you have to complete more than one project in the year, it is particularly important to produce a list or a chart indicating the stage at which all data should have been collected, analysis carried out and writing begun. Delay on one project means that the timing for the second and third will be upset. It is immaterial whether you produce a list or a chart, but some attempt at planning progress should be attempted.

One of the most common reasons for falling behind is that reading takes longer than anticipated. Books and articles have to be located, and the temptation to read just one more book is strong. At some stage a decision has to be made to stop reading, no matter how inadequate the coverage of the subject is. Forcing yourself to move on is a discipline that has to be learnt. Keep in touch with your supervisor about progress.

If things go wrong and you are held up on one stage, there may be other ways of overcoming the problem. Talk about it. Ask for help and advice *before* you become weeks out of phase with your timetable, so that you have a chance of amending your original project plan. The project outline is for guidance only. If subsequent events indicate that it would be better to ask different questions and even to have a different aim, then change while there is time. You have to work to the date specified by the institution, and your supervisor and external examiner will understand that.

Planning the Project Checklist

1. Draw up a short list of topics.

    Consult library catalogues, colleagues and fellow students.

2. Select a topic for investigation.

    Discuss possible outcomes with your supervisor and decide what the emphasis of your study is to be.

3. Establish the precise focus of the study.

    Draw up 'first thoughts' list of questions and subject each to rigorous examination.

4. Decide on the aims and objectives of the study or formulate a hypothesis.

    Think carefully about what is and what is not worth investigating.

5. Draw up an initial project outline.

List aims and/or objectives, questions to be investigated, possible methods of investigation and literature to be consulted.

6. Read enough to enable you to decide whether you are on the right lines.

This initial reading may give you ideas about approach and methods and how information might be classified.

7. Devise a timetable to enable you to check that all stages will be covered and time allowed for writing.

It is easy to take too long over one stage and so to have insufficient time to carry out essential tasks in the next stage.

8. Consult your supervisor.

At the stage of deciding on a topic, and after drawing up an initial project outline.

STUDY CHAPTER 3 BEFORE YOU BEGIN
YOUR PRELIMINARY READING.

3

Reviewing the Literature

Any investigation, whatever the scale, will involve reading what other people have written about your area of interest, gathering information to support or refute your arguments and writing about your findings. In a small-scale project, you will not be expected to produce a definitive account of the state of research in your selected topic area, but you will need to provide evidence that you have read a certain amount of relevant literature and that you have some awareness of the current state of knowledge on the subject.

Ideally, the bulk of your reading should come early in the investigation, though in practice a number of activities are generally in progress at the same time and reading may even spill over into the data collecting stage of your study. As indicated in the last chapter, you need to take care that reading does not take up more time than can be allowed, but it is rarely possible to obtain copies of all books and articles at exactly the time you need them, so there is inevitably some overlap.

Analytical and Theoretical Frameworks

Reading as much as time permits about your topic may give you ideas about approach and methods which had not occurred to you and may also give you ideas about how you might classify and present your own data. It may help you to devise a theoretical or analytical framework as a basis for the analysis and interpretation of data. It is not enough merely to collect facts and to describe what is. All researchers collect many facts, but then must organize and classify them into a coherent pattern. Verma and Beard (1981) suggest that researchers need to

> identify and explain relevant relationships between the facts. In other words, the researcher must produce a concept or build a theoretical structure that can explain facts and the relationships between them . . . The importance of theory is to help the investigator summarize previous information and guide his future course of action. Sometimes the formulation of a theory may indicate missing ideas or links and the kinds of additional data required. Thus, a theory is an essential tool of research in stimulating the advancement of knowledge still further.
>
> (Verma and Beard 1981:10)

Sometimes 'model' is used instead of or interchangeably with 'theory'. Cohen and Manion explain that

> both may be seen as explanatory devices or schemes having a conceptual framework, though models are often characterized by the use of analogies to give a more graphic or visual representation of a particular phenomenon. Providing they are accurate and do not misrepresent the facts, models can be of great help in achieving clarity and focusing on key issues in the nature of phenomena.

> (Cohen and Manion 1980:18)

The label is not important but the process of ordering and classifying data is.

As you read, get into the habit of examining how authors classify their findings, how they explore relationships between facts and how facts and relationships are explained. Methods used by other researchers may be unsuitable for your purposes, but they may give you ideas about how you might categorize your own data, and ways in which you may be able to draw on the work of other researchers to support or refute your own arguments and conclusions.

The Critical Review of the Literature

An extensive study of the literature will be required in most cases for a PhD and a critical review of what has been written on the topic produced in the final thesis. A project lasting two or three months will not require anything so ambitious. You may decide to omit an initial review altogether if your reading has not been sufficiently extensive to warrant its inclusion, but if you decide to produce a review, it is important to remember that only relevant works are mentioned and that the review is more than a list of 'what I have read'.

Writing literature reviews can be a demanding exercise. Haywood and Wragg comment wryly that critical reviews are more often than not uncritical reviews — what they describe as

> the furniture sale catalogue, in which everything merits a one-paragraph entry no matter how skilfully it has been conducted: Bloggs (1975) found this, Smith (1976) found that, Jones (1977) found the other, Bloggs, Smith and Jones (1978) found happiness in heaven.

> (Haywood and Wragg 1982:2)

They go on to say that a critical review should show 'that the writer has studied existing work in the field with insight' (p.2). That is easier said than done, but the main point to bear in mind is that a review should provide the reader with a picture, albeit limited in a short project, of the state of knowledge and of major questions in the subject area being investigated.

Consider the following introduction to a study by Alan Woodley (1985) entitled *Taking Account of Mature Students*. You may not be familiar with this field of study, but does the introduction put you in the picture? Does it give you some idea of the work that has been done already and does it prepare you for what is to follow?

Of the many who have looked at the relationship between age and performance in universities none has as yet produced a definite answer to the apparently simple question 'Do mature students do better or worse than younger students?'

Harris (1940) in the United States found evidence to suggest that younger students tended to obtain better degree results. Similar findings have been made in Britain by Malleson (1959), Forster (1959), Howell (1962), Barnett and Lewis (1963), McCracken (1969) and Kapur (1972), in Australia by Flecker (1959) and Sanders (1961), in Canada by Fleming (1959), and in New Zealand by Small (1966). However, most of these studies were based on samples of students who were generally aged between seventeen and twenty-one and the correlation techniques employed meant that the relationship between age and performance really only concerned this narrow age band. As such, the results probably suggest that bright children admitted early to higher education fare better than those whose entry is delayed while they gain the necessary qualifications. This view is supported by Harris (1940) who discovered that the relationship between age and performance disappeared when he controlled for intelligence. Other studies have shown that those who gain the necessary qualifications and then delay entry for a year or two are more successful than those who enter directly from school (Thomas, Beeby and Oram 1939; Derbyshire Education Committee 1966; Orr 1974).

Where studies have involved samples containing large numbers of older students the results have indicated that the relationship between age and performance is not a linear one. Philips and Cullen (1955), for instance, found that those aged twenty-four and over tended to do better than the eighteen and nineteen-year-old age group. Sanders (1961) showed that the university success rate fell until the age of twenty or twenty-one, then from about twenty-two onwards the success rate began to rise again. The problem with these two studies is that many of the older students were returning servicemen. They were often 'normal' entrants whose entry to university had been delayed by war and many had undergone some training in science or mathematics while in the armed forces. Also, while Eaton (1980) cites nine American studies which confirm the academic superiority of veterans, there is some contradictory British evidence. Mountford (1957) found that ex-service students who entered Liverpool University between 1947 and 1949 were more likely to have to spend an extra year or more on their courses and more likely to fail to complete their course.

Some studies have shown that whether mature students fare better or worse than younger students depends upon the subject being studied. Sanders (1963) has indicated that the maturity associated with increasing age and experience seems to be a positive predictor of success for some arts and social science courses. The general finding that older students do better in arts and social science and worse in science and maths is supported by Barnett, Holder and Lewis (1968), Fagin (1971), Sharon (1971) and Flecker (1959).

Walker's (1975) study of mature students at Warwick University represents the best British attempt to unravel the relationship between age and performance. He took 240 mature undergraduates who were admitted to the university between 1965 and 1971 and compared their progress with that of all undergraduates. This gave him a reasonably large sample to work with and the timing meant that the results were not distorted by any 'returning servicemen factor'. His methodology showed certain other refinements. First, he excluded overseas students. Such students tend to be older than average and also to fare worse academically (Woodley 1979), thus influencing any age/performance relationship. Secondly, he used two measures of performance; the proportion leaving without obtaining a degree and the degree results of those taking final examinations. Finally he weighted the degree class obtained according to its rarity value in each faculty.

The following findings achieved statistical significance:

(i)   In total, mature students obtained better degrees than non-mature students.

(ii) In the arts faculty mature students obtained better degrees than non-mature students.

(iii) Mature students who did not satisfy the general entrance requirement obtained better degrees than all other students.

(iv) The degree results of mature students aged twenty-six to thirty were better than those of all other mature students.

Several other differences were noted but they did not achieve statistical significance due to the small numbers involved. The mature student sample only contained thirty-three women, twenty-six science students and thirty-seven aged over thirty. The aim of the present study was to extend Walker's work to all British universities so that these and other relationships could be tested out on a much larger sample of mature students.

(Woodley 1985: 152–4).

This review is more thorough than would normally be required for small projects, but the approach is much the same, whatever the size of the exercise. Alan Woodley selects from the extensive amount of literature relating to mature students. He groups certain categories and comments on features which are of particular interest. He compares results of different investigators and discusses in some detail a study by Walker (1975) which serves as a pilot for his more extensive study of mature students in British universities.

The reader is then in the picture and has some understanding of what work has been done already in this field. Woodley no doubt omitted many publications that had been consulted during the course of his research. It is always hard to leave out publications that may have taken you many hours or even weeks to read, but the selection has to be made.

Locating Published Materials

If you are provided with a topic for investigation, then you will in all probability be given lists of books and articles which come under the heading of Required Reading, Recommended Reading, Suggested Reading, Set Books, or something of the kind. That is obviously your starting point, and in a small project which has to be completed in two or three months, may provide sufficient reading for your purposes. If you are selecting your own topic, you will need to find out what has been published in your field, even if time only allows you to read a selection of books, articles and reviews. It is important

1. To find the most relevant published materials quickly.
2. To avoid getting bogged down.
3. To get into the habit of recording information derived from your reading so that it can be easily found and understood weeks, months or years later.

Earlier chapters in this book have stressed the need to adopt a systematic approach to planning an investigation. Whatever the size of the task, the same meticulous planning and attention to detail needs to be adopted in conducting a literature search. The first step is to ensure that you fully understand the services that are offered by library staff, and what materials the library holds — on the shelves, in reserve collections, on microfiche or microfilm. Bibliographies, abstracts, indexes and encyclopedias can save hours of searching for sources, but they are not always easy to find or to understand. Although most libraries in this country follow the Dewey decimal system of classification, libraries do have different views about how some publications should be classified and stored. Government publications are notoriously difficult to find in a library which is new to you, and rather than waste valuable time tracing them, it may be best to ask at the library information desk and to seek expert advice at an early stage. All libraries vary to some extent, so some time needs to be invested to become familiar with the geography and the stock before you begin your search for the literature. But first find your library.

Access to Libraries

Public Libraries

The services of public libraries in the local authority where you live (and possibly also where you work) will be available free of charge, and a good many local authorities have arrangements with neighbouring authorities which allow you to have borrowing rights. Small branch libraries will not generally have stocks which will be of use to research workers, though in some cases special collections have been built up which are of great value to students. Eastwood library in Nottinghamshire, for example, has a good collection of works by and relating to D.H. Lawrence, who lived in Eastwood at one time. However, this is rather exceptional, and generally speaking an investigator will need to make use of the large main libraries.

Academic Libraries

If you are a registered university, polytechnic or college student you will normally have full borrowing rights for your institution's library. 'Outsiders' who wish to use the facilities of an academic library will need to obtain the librarian's permission. Some libraries will give permission for bona fide students to use the library for reference purposes, and a generous few allow lending facilities. However, you cannot *demand* to use specialist libraries. They are for the use of the students and staff of the institution and demands made on library staff are likely to stretch their resources and patience, particularly at certain times of the year. Teachers and others engaged in educational work in England, Wales and Northern Ireland are generally entitled to use the libraries of their nearest school or institute of education, though again this may be restricted to reference use, and in recent years a number of institute libraries have been incorporated into main university libraries.

What Are You Looking For?

We all think we know how to use libraries, and certainly it would not take any of us long to get to grips with the system operating and the stock held by small branch libraries. Finding the way round and discovering what stock is held in main public and specialist libraries in universities, polytechnics and colleges is quite another matter. They can seem like Aladdin's caves for students and researchers. They hold treasures that dazzle; but caves can be dangerous. It is easy to get lost and to become so anxious not to leave any of the treasures behind that it becomes impossible ever to leave. All this is rather fanciful, but many a research project has foundered because the investigator had not defined the area of study sufficiently clearly and so extended the range of reading far beyond what was necessary. Large libraries are complicated places, and library staff at the information desk will do their best to help you to come to grips with the way the stock is organized — but first, you need to know *exactly* what you are looking for.

You will only really get to know what a library can offer and how to use the facilities when you start looking for information yourself. Discussing library use in the abstract means very little until you are on the trail yourself, but there are certain guidelines that will help you to plan a search and certain steps that need to be taken whatever the scale of the operation. Planning a literature search demands certain skills, foremost amongst which is the ability to define precisely what you mean. Let us say your area of interest is *leadership*. That would be your starting point, but exactly what do you mean by leadership? How will the library classify works which relate to leadership? Are you interested in leadership in schools, in the steel industry or in government? Do you want references as far back as possible, or only in the past two years? In the UK, worldwide, or only in Halifax? Are there likely to be books and articles of interest to you that are classified under different headings? In fact, what do you mean and what exactly are you looking for?

The following outline takes you through the process of planning. If you are not to waste time, this process needs to be carried out whether you are intending to conduct a large and complex computer search or whether your time and resources limit you to a study of library holdings and a range of other secondary sources (bibliographies, abstracts, indexes, etc.).

Planning a Literature Search

	Examples
1. *Select the topic*	Leadership.
2. *Define the terminology*	Leadership may be sufficient at this stage, but before you continue, do you have a clear idea of what 'leadership' means? Might other countries use a different terminology? If you consider the term 'leadership' is sufficiently explicit, continue to the next stage.
3. *Define parameters*	
— Language	English?
— Geography	Material published in the UK only? USA? Australia? Where else? (If you only have two or three months to complete the entire project, you can't do everything. Keep the literature search to the UK and only move overseas if the search reveals nothing of significance).
— Time period	1980 to the present?
— Type of material	Journals, books, theses? (You may not have time to consult theses, which are generally only available for reference or on inter-library loan).
— Sector	School? Further education? University?

4. *List possible search terms*

The term 'leadership' is unlikely to produce all the relevant sources. You need to think of synonyms under which works of interest to you might have been classified. It may be helpful to consult a dictionary, or *Roget's Thesaurus* for ideas. Think of alternatives to 'leadership', or headings which might include aspects of leadership (authority? head teacher? manager?). One approach is to produce a diagram on the lines of Figure 3.1, but you may find it easier simply to list all the terms you can think of. Remember, your diagram or list will probably expand as the search proceeds.

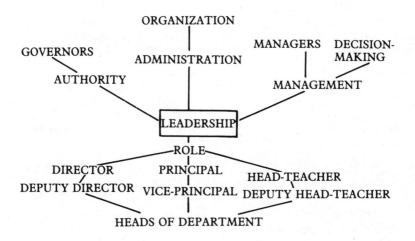

Figure 3.1 The search for terms.

Having selected the topic, defined the terminology and the parameters, selected the research terms and put them into alphabetical order, you are then in a position to start looking for the materials. Your next step is to select sources.

5. *Select sources*
   Library catalogue

Use the subject approach with selected terms (leadership, management, authority, head-teacher, etc.). Make a note of the appropriate library class numbers.

You can then use the classified catalogue, which is in class number order (i.e. in the same order as the books on the shelves) to find out exactly what the library holds on a particular subject. The library catalogue can be consulted again later as further search terms emerge from the bibliographies. You will also need to return to it at the end of your literature search, using an author or title approach, to check whether the library holds any material you discover in the bibliographies and which was missed in your original subject search.

Bibliographies

These will provide you with brief references of published works in your area. Start with books.

(a) Books

The *British National Bibliography (BNB)* has been published since 1950 and is generally available for consultation in public libraries. There are cumulative volumes. Use the index, which will probably list other terms you have not yet thought of. List these, to ensure consistency when searching through each *BNB* volume. (*BNB* also covers first issues of journals, monographs and some government publications, but it is concerned mainly with books.)

The following extracts illustrate the way in which *BNB* lists items under subject headings.

From BNB Index

(Volume 1, 1980)

Primary Schools

372.1'2'0120926 — **Primary schools. Head-teachers. Leadership.** *United States. Case studies*
Jentz, Barry C. Leadership and learning : personal change in a professional setting / [by] Barry C. Jentz and Joan W. Wofford. — New York ; London [etc.] : McGraw-Hill, 1979. — xv,181,[1]p ; 24cm.
ISBN 0-07-032497-2 : £6.10

(B80-01592)

**372.1'2'0120941 — Primary schools. Head-teachers.
Role.** *Great Britain*
Jones, Roy. Primary school management / [by]
Roy Jones. — Newton Abbot [etc.] : David and
Charles, 1980. — 159p : 3 ill ; 23cm.
Bibl.: p.155. — Index.
ISBN 0-7153-7843-0 : £4.95 : CIP rev.

(B79-35781)

**372.1'2'0120942 — Primary schools. Head-teachers
Role.** *England*
Waters, Derek. Management and headship in the
primary school / [by] Derek Waters. —
London : Ward Lock, 1979. — vi,338p : ill,
forms ; 22cm.
Bibl.: p.330-335. — Index.
ISBN 0-7062-3865-6 Pbk : £5.95

(B80-24346)

Schools Administration

371.2'00941 — Schools. Administration. *Great
Britain*
John, Denys. Leadership in schools. — London :
Heinemann Educational, May 1980. — [196]p.
— (Organisation in schools)
ISBN 0-435-80468-5 : £8.00 : CIP entry

(B80-05844

**371.2'012'0722 — Schools Administration. Role of
head teachers.** *United States. Case
studies*
Blumberg, Arthur. The effective principal :
perspectives on school leadership / [by] Arthur
Blumberg, William Greenfield. — Boston, Mass
(London [*etc.*]) : Allyn and Bacon, 1980. —
viii,280p ; 25cm.
Bibl.: p.271-273. — Index.
ISBN 0-205-06812-x : £15.95

(B80-25433)

From BNB Subject Catalogue
(Volume 2, 1980)

Head teachers

Head-teachers. Primary schools. England
    Role   372.1'2'0120942
Head-teachers. Primary schools. Great Britain
    Role   372.1'2'0120941
Head-teachers. Primary schools. United States
    Leadership — *Case studies*   372.1'2'0120926
Head-teachers. Schools. United States
    Role in administration — *Case studies*
                                   371.2'012'0722
Head-teachers. Secondary schools. United States
    Administration duties   373.1'2'0120973

Leadership

Leadership
See also
   Captaincy. Sports
Leadership
   — *Conference proceedings*   301.15'53
Leadership. Christian life   248
Leadership. Discussion groups
   Christian life — *Daily readings — For discussion*
     group leadership — Serials   242'.2'05
Leadership. Group work. Roman Catholic Church
                                   267
Leadership. Head-teachers. Primary schools. United
   States — *Case studies*   372.1'2'0120926
Leadership. Management
   — *Manuals*   658.4
Leadership. Management. Teams. Business firms
   — *Manuals — For construction industries* 658.4'02
Leadership. Politics. Great Britain
   1916-1978. Psychology   301.5'92
Leadership. Students. Schools
   Assessment. Sociometric analysis — *For teaching*
                              371.8'1

You will note that the Dewey decimal number is given in these *BNB* extracts. When you look up this number in *BNB's* classified sequence you will find the full bibliographical details of the work indexed. It is important to use the index and find the Dewey number for each year of *BNB* that you search, because class numbers change and also vary according to the subject emphasis. As you scan the items, you will note that some do not fulfil your stipulated criteria. Two of the above items are published in the USA. It would be foolish to suggest that once you have defined parameters, you may not move outside them, but bibliographies and indexes make seductive reading. Titles look interesting, and before you know it, every title in the bibliography is noted. Try to discipline yourself and take the view that a strong case has to be made for the inclusion of any publication which falls outside your stipulated limits. Remind yourself how much time you can afford on this literature search and the reading which will inevitably follow, and be ruthless.

Having scanned the *BNB* for books, you move on to journals.

(b) journals

British Education Index (BEI) has been published since 1954, with annual cumulative volumes. *BEI* indexes British periodicals concerned with education, and all the details necessary for finding an article on a particular topic are given in the subject list. Remember you are not checking under 'leadership' alone. You will also need to check under your other search terms.

The following extracts illustrate the way in which BEI lists some of the terms which are associated with the topic of 'leadership'.

Leadership

LEADERSHIP. Classroom behaviour. Teachers
The **teacher's** leadership behaviour in the classroom / Shizuo Yoshizaki. — *Sch. Psychol. Int.*, Vol.1, no.5 : 81. — p13-14

LEADERSHIP. Higher education institutions
Style
Leadership styles in institutions of higher education : a contingency approach / O.A. Ajayi. — *Coombe Lodge Rep.*, Vol.14, no.4 : 81. — p211-222
Bibliography: p221-222

LEADERSHIP. Managers
Training
Leadership development — towards an interpersonal skills training programme / Beverly Alban Metcalfe. — *J. Eur. Ind. Train.*, Vol.5, no.1 : 81. — p23-26

LEADERSHIP. Principals. Further education institutions
Sustaining leadership / Eric Briault. — *Coombe Lodge Rep.*, Vol.14, no.3 : 81. — p172-178

Management

MANAGEMENT. Primary schools
1967-1980 — Ireland & Northern Ireland — Comparative studies
The **implementation** of changes in the managerial system in primary schools in Northern Ireland and the Republic of Ireland, 1967-1980 : a comparative study / Michael McKeown. — *Ir. Educ. Stud.*, Vol.1 : 81. — p275-295

MANAGEMENT. Recreation facilities. Community schools
The **management** of recreational facilities in community schools / Michael McDonough. — *Ir. Educ. Stud.*, Vol.1 : 81. — p376-394
Bibliography: p393-394

MANAGEMENT. Schools
Decision making. Participation of teachers. Attitudes of trainee teachers
Personal variables in student-teacher attitudes towards teacher participation in school decision-making / G.A. Richardson. — *Durham Newcastle Res. Rev.*, Vol.9, no.47 : Autumn 81. — p285-291

Deputy head-teachers

DEPUTY HEAD-TEACHERS. Primary schools
In-service training. Courses — Case studies
Primary school management : an in-service course / B.J. Leatherbarrow. — *Br. J. In-serv. Educ.*, Vol.7, no.3 : Summer 81. — p176-178

(c) abstracts

Abstracts are invaluable and can save weeks of effort, so it is always worth investigating what is available. They provide summaries of books, articles, etc. *School Organization and Management Abstracts* has been produced quarterly since 1982 and is available for reference in major libraries. Research into *Higher Education Abstracts* is produced by the Society for Research into Higher Education. *Sociology of Education Abstracts*, published by Carfax Publishing Company has been produced since 1965 and a number of American and Canadian abstracting services provide international coverage of books, journals, reports, etc.

You can find out what abstracts are available in your area of interest by consulting *Ulrich's International Periodicals Directory,* and library staff will tell you which abstracts are in stock.

(d) Theses

The *British Education Theses Index 1950–1980* (*BETI*) provides information on microfiche on a subject basis. Most theses can be obtained through inter-library loan, but this always takes time and involves a charge. If you are preparing for a higher degree, it is important to give yourself an idea of style, format, length, etc., but if you are working on a more limited project, you may not have time to spend obtaining and reading theses.

The above outline does not include many of the sources that are available to a researcher, but it is likely to be sufficient for most individual investigators working within a limited time scale and with little or no funding. If you wish to know more, there are many publications to help you. Dale and Carty (1985) in *Finding Out about Continuing Education: Sources of Information and Their Use* and Haywood and Wragg (1982) in *Evaluating the Literature* produce an extensive range of information about bibliographies, glossaries, encyclopedias, reviews, indexes, abstracts, current-awareness services, theses and a good deal more. Haywood and Wragg also give guidance about using a computer link to retrieve information. You will only need to make use of a computer search if you need to conduct a very thorough study of the literature. If you or your institution can afford computer searches, they will reveal sources quickly, but they may produce more information then you can deal with in the time available. They require the help of library staff, can only be conducted where the library has access to a terminal, and they cost money. You can quickly run up a large bill, particularly if your enthusiasm gets the better of you. Valuable though computer searches are, most small-scale investigators will still depend on the library catalogue to locate sources.

Obtaining the Materials

The indexes, bibliographies and catalogues will provide you with information about what is available, but the next step is to obtain the books and articles relating to your area of interest. Return to the library catalogue to find out what is in stock and where, either on the library shelves, in a reserve store or on microfiche. A brief scan can sometimes be enough to tell you whether the book or article is likely to be worth thorough study. Look at the preface and the chapter headings and see if there are summaries to chapters. Journal articles will generally have brief abstracts which give a clear idea of content and approach. If the material is not in stock, you may have to order it on inter-library loan, but remember that this is not a free service. Either you or your library will have to pay, so make sure you have exhausted all the sources in your own library before you turn to outside stocks and check the information you have about the material before placing the order. Look at the date of publication. Is it likely to have been superseded? Does the reference in the bibliography or index give any clues? Might it relate to a context sufficiently different from your own to make it of only marginal interest? Have you seen a reference to this book or article in another work? Checks of this kind are unlikely to be foolproof, but they can help in drawing up a short list of requirements.

It is often worrying to know whether enough reading has been done in connection with a particular project. It is impossible to read everything, or you would never get down to the task of collecting and analysing data. You might end with an impressive review but nothing else. Keep an eye on your schedule, and if you are falling behind, amend your reading plans. Your supervisor will provide guidance about what constitutes accepted practice in your institution, and if you seem to be spending too long on background reading, will no doubt tell you to stop and to move the project a stage further.

If your referencing is well done and if you make careful notes of your reading as you go along, you are preparing part of your literature review and so part of your final report. Examine your notes carefully. Ask yourself what the book or article contributes to the field you are studying and, while the material is fresh in your mind, try to draft a review of what you have read. But before you begin your programme of reading, study the next chapter and decide exactly how you are going to record your sources and categorize your evidence. It is important to get the nuts and bolts of referencing and recording sorted and good practice established.

Reviewing the Literature Checklist

1. All investigations require evidence of reading.

   You may get ideas about methods of data collection and analysis.

2. A critical review of the literature may not be necessary for small projects, but if a review is produced, it should include only relevant items.

   The review should provide the reader with a picture of the state of knowledge in the subject.

3. Locate your nearest library and negotiate access.

   Take advantage of any library guides or slide–tape programmes of library services.

4. Decide exactly what you need to know before you begin your literature search.

5. Select the topic.

6. Define the terminology.

   Think of synonyms.

7. Define the parameters.

   1980 to the present? UK materials only?

8. Select sources.

   Library catalogues, bibliographies, *BNB, BEI*, abstracts, indexes, etc.

9. Locate appropriate materials.

10. Write up as you go along.

    You are preparing for the review at this stage. Note methods of investigation, methods of classifying data and items of particular information for your investigation.

> EVERYTHING THAT IS READ HAS TO BE RECORDED. READ THE NEXT CHAPTER BEFORE YOU BEGIN TO READ FOR YOUR PROJECT

4

Keeping Records and Making Notes

Finding information in the first place can be hard enough. Finding it again some time afterwards can be even harder unless your methods of recording and filing are thorough and systematic. We all think we shall remember, but after several weeks of reading, analysing and selecting, memory becomes faulty. After a few months, we may vaguely recall having read something some time about the topic being studied, but when and where escapes us. After a longer period, the chances of remembering are remote. So, everything that is read must be noted, and the sooner some systematic system of record-keeping is started, the better.

It may seem a waste of time to record a source which proves to be of no use or interest, but there must have been some reason why you decided to look at it in the first place. The title may have sounded interesting, or you may have read other works by the same author that impressed you. It would follow then that some time ahead, the title may still sound interesting and the author may still be remembered as having produced quality work in another context. You may come across the reference again, and ask to borrow the book again. All this is a waste of time, and in any investigation, whether small or large scale, there is never enough time to do everything that has to be done. A note to remind you why you decided the work was of no interest would be enough to jog your memory and to enable you to abandon that particular line of inquiry.

The Card Index

In the early days of an investigation it may seem enough to jot down a reference on the back of an envelope, but old envelopes thrown into a box will not provide you with a reliable resource, and the likelihood is that references will be incomplete and difficult to track down at a later stage. It you are only going to need half a dozen references, then scraps of paper may serve, but as your investigation proceeds, you will accumulate many sources of information, and an orderly system is necesary from the beginning. Most research workers will acknowledge that they have wasted valuable time tracing books, periodicals, quotations because they forgot to note the reference at the time, or because they inexplicably left off the name of the journal, the author or the date. The advantage of cards is that you can insert later entries and can re-sort if necessary. You can use the 5″ × 3″ size cards normally used in library catalogues, the 6″ × 4″ size, or the 8″ × 5″, which give more room for notes. It is a case of personal preference, but once you have chosen one size of card, stick to it.

The cards should be complete references and should include all the information you are likely to need for inter-library loan applications and for drawing up the references or bibliography for your project report. They may include brief notes about the content of the book or article and reminders that a certain chapter or page had useful information about some topic. They will be your stock-in-trade, and you should start building up your stock as soon as you begin your studies.

You will always require the following information:

Books	*Articles*
Author's surname and forename or initials	Author's surname and forename or initials
Date of publication	Date of publication
Title (underlined)	Title (in inverted commas)
Place of publication	Source of the article, namely:
Publisher	Title of journal (underlined)
	Volume
	Issue and page numbers

Titles of books and articles are not abbreviated, but titles of journals may be. Bibliographies normally abbreviate in the standard way the titles they list, but you can check the *British Education Index* for the standard abbreviation of most of the journals you are likely to use. If journals you are using are not listed in the *British Educational Index*, the *British Standards Institution* (BS) 4148 (usually available for consultation in libraries) sets out the conventions, and you can then work out an abbreviation for yourself. Do not make up your own abbreviations; so if in doubt reproduce the title in full.

It may not be necessary to include all the information found on library catalogue cards and on *BNB* references. Consider the information on the following *BNB* entry, in Figure 4.1. What information do you need from this entry? You will obviously need the author, the title of the book, the place of publication, name of publisher and date of publication. You may feel it is of little importance to remember that this book has 159 pages, but the price may be useful, if you or the library wish to purchase a copy of the book. The ISBN number (International Standard Book Number), which is a number unique to the publication concerned, is useful if you are requesting a book on inter-library loan, so it is worth adding to your card. You may not feel it is of much interest to know that the bibliography appears on page 155, nor that there is an index. The Dewey decimal number should only be recorded from the catalogue in your own library, so there would be no reason to transfer the number from a *BNB* entry, but you may need to know where you originally found the book, in case you need to consult it again, so the source of reference should be noted (e.g. *BNB* 1979, *BEI* 1986, Sheffield University catalogue, etc.).

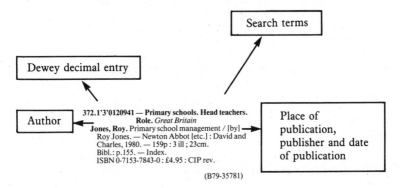

Figure 4.1 *BNB* entry sample.

Referencing

There are a number of perfectly acceptable ways of recording sources and other information, and most educational institutions will have a preferred 'house' style which you will be expected to adopt. If no guidance is provided, or if you are left to decide yourself, you will need to consider which of the available options suits you best. The two most commonly used methods of referencing used in this country are the British and the Harvard methods.

The British system, which is based on the British Standards Institution, places the author's initials or forename before the surname, and the date appears after the volume, part or issue number (for journals) and after the publisher (for books), as follows:

M. Bassey. 'Pedagogic Research: On the Relative Merits of Search for Generalisation and Study of Single Events'. *Oxford Review of Education* 7 (1), 73–94 (1981).

Sheila Dale and Joan Carty. *Finding Out about Continuing Education: Sources of Information and Their Use*. Milton Keynes, Open University Press, 1985.

The disadvantage of this method is that when works are referred to in the main body of the text, references have to be supplied either by

means of footnotes (which make difficulties for typists), or by end notes. In the main text, for example, the Dale and Carty reference would appear as follows:
'Dale and Carty, in their discussion of bibliographical tools . . .'[1] and at the end of the chapter or in a footnote, as follows:

---

1. Sheila Dale and Joan Carty *Finding Out about Continuing Education: Sources of Information and Their Use.* Milton Keynes, Open University Press, 1985, p. 21.

The Harvard method, which I use in this book, has a number of advantages over the British system. It avoids footnotes, does not interrupt the flow of the text and yet provides information for the reader about sources without the necessity of referring to end notes. The principle is that in the text the author's surname and date of publication is included; for example, 'As Dale and Carty (1985) say . . .' The full details of Dale and Carty's 1985 publication will then appear in the alphabetical list at the end of the chapter or report. Page references are given in the text for any quotations or where the writer is drawing heavily on another writer's ideas.

As I have said, sources appear in alphabetical order at the end of the chapter or report, not in the order in which they appear in the text. If an author has more than one entry, then the publications are listed in chronological order. If an author has more than one publication in the same year, then suffixes 'a' or 'b' are added, for example, Youngman (1979a) and Youngman (1979b). Where more than one author is involved, the first name determines the order.

The Harvard method of referencing provides a simple way of coping with references in the main text and also in bibliographies. However, as long as you are consistent throughout and follow a recognized method, it does not matter which style you select. Referencing can take an irritatingly long time if you have to keep checking back, so good habits established early in your investigations will pay off later on. If your cards are in good order, drawing up your bibliography will only be a matter of transferring the information from card to paper, but it must be done in a consistent way. It is not permissible to use the Harvard system for one reference, the British system for another and a method of your own for a third.

It takes a little time to remember all the detail of what is underlined and what appears in inverted commas, where dates appear and how to deal with quotations. Once you have mastered the detail, it becomes automatic to record *all* sources as soon as you come across them, *in the format of your choice.* Because the detail is difficult to remember, it is wise to keep model cards for your card index to remind you what should always be included and also to keep an example of a list of references in a published work, so that you can check that your punctuation and detail are consistent. Something on the lines shown in Figure 4.2 would serve the purpose quite well.

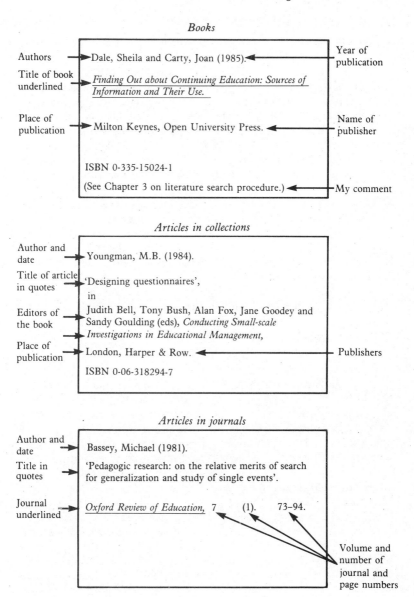

Figure 4.2 Model reference format for books, articles in collections and articles in journals.

Note-taking and Preparation for the Report

In addition to recording bibliographical details, you will need to devise a system of note-taking which records the actual evidence obtained from your sources. Some researchers prefer notebooks, some prefer loose sheets of paper and others prefer note cards. If you use a notebook, information will be recorded as it is obtained but leave a wide margin blank to insert categories later. At a later stage you may wish to cut up the notebook, preferably into pieces of uniform size, to enable you to sort evidence into categories and sections ready for planning the format of your report.

Whether you use notebooks, loose sheets or note cards will depend on your preference, but the type of information you record and the method of recording will be the same. There is some merit in selecting cards. They are easy to sort and to reclassify: they are all the same size and so easy to handle and they are likely to stand up well to wear and tear. Experience has shown that it is best to make only one point on each card and to use only one side of the paper or card. You will then have maximum flexibility in sorting out the cards at the writing stage.

The Categorization of Evidence

All your preliminary work is leading up to the writing of your report or dissertation. If you have already mapped out chapter or topic headings, you will have the basis of a system of categorization of evidence. If not, categories will emerge as you read. Your first choice of categories when recording information may in any case prove to be unsuitable, and alterations may be needed as your understanding of the subject grows, so write the subject key in the left-hand corner of the card in pencil at first (the rest of the card should be typed or written in ink), so it can easily be recategorized if necessary.

Sorting the cards into categories will help shape the report's structure. At the writing stage they can be placed in the order in which the points will be made and divided into small manageable sections ready to be written up. Examples of the kind of categories that might be used in an investigation of the management of staff for example are: Staff selection; staff promotion; staff appraisal; INSET; secondment; non-teaching staff; funding; career patterns; induction; institutional policy. If certain sources are going to be used frequently, a key for the note cards can be devised to speed up the recording of information. If, for example, a particular government report was an important source for a project, it could be given a number which would go in the right-hand corner of the card with the volume and page numbers. You would then, of course, need to make a careful record of the numbers — perhaps also on cards which could be kept in numerical order.

Figure 4.3 gives an example of a note card for a project on open-learning methods which records a point about the Open Tech from *The Times Educational Supplement.* Try to paraphrase the information as much as possible. This not only gives practice in the art of writing but it makes note-making more creative and it will make the final writing easier (Barzun and Graff 1977:24).

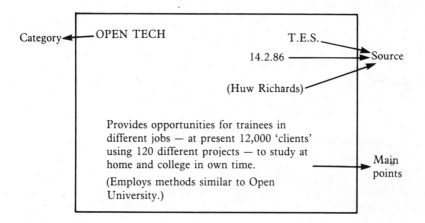

Figure 4.3 Example of a note card.

Noting Quotations

A particularly perceptive observation by an author may often illustrate a point you wish to make in an assignment or report, and add an extra dimension to your argument. Making a note of quotations at the time you read them is as important as recording the full bibliographical information about the source. When you are writing up your final report, you will not have time to recall books from the library, nor to search in the used envelope box. If a particular sentence or paragraph strikes you at the time of reading as being a potential quotation, note it carefully, record the chapter and page number, show clearly if you have left out any word or words by adding three full stops, and file it where you know you will be able to find it, even if this requires some cross-referencing in your card index. If you have the facilities, it is an even better idea to photocopy the extract, adding details about source in the usual way, and attaching it to your card. (Library staff will advise about copyright regulations.) If you are unable to photocopy, then make it quite clear which is the quotation and which is your paraphrase, or when you come to write up your project you may find you are committing the sin of using someone else's words as your own.

A Lot of Fuss about Nothing?

Well no. Just acquiring the tools of the trade. Referencing can be irritatingly pernickety, but once you have established a routine, recording information becomes automatic and no problem at all. If you assimilate the information in this chapter and if you record your sources accurately and consistently, you will have begun to establish good research habits and to lay the foundations of your own research. You will be rewarded for your hard work, if not in heaven, then certainly when you come to write your report. You will be able to locate information easily, to regroup and reclassify evidence and to produce quotations to support your arguments. If your card index is in good shape, preparing a bibliography or list of references for your report will merely be a matter of sorting cards into alphabetical order. And what could be easier than that?

Keeping Records and Making Notes Checklist

1. Make a note of everything you read.	Even note the items that were no use.
2. Start a card index as soon as you begin your investigation.	Select a card size and stick to it.
3. When recording sources, make sure you always note author's name and initials, date of publication, title (underlined for books, in inverted commas for articles), place of publication and publisher.	There are variations for books, articles in collections and journal articles. Make out model cards as memory joggers.
4. Decide on a system of referencing and stick to it.	The British and Harvard systems are the most commonly used in this country.
5. Decide whether to use a notebook, loose sheets or cards for note-taking.	Use one side of paper or cards to ease sorting.
6. Devise a 'first thoughts' list of categories.	Devise a subject key, if necessary. Write the categories and/or key in pencil in case changes are needed later on.

7. Make an accurate note of all quotations at the time you read them.

Note whether any omissions (by . . .); make clear what is a direct quotation and what is your paraphrase. Photocopy extracts if possible — then you know there are no errors.

8. Whatever method and format you adopt, BE CONSISTENT.

5

Negotiating Access and the Problems of 'Inside' Research

No researcher can demand access to an institution, an organization or to materials. People will be doing you a favour if they agree to help, and they will need to know exactly what they will be asked to do, how much time they will be expected to give and what use will be made of the information they provide. Teachers, administrators, parents and keepers of documents will have to be convinced of your integrity and of the value of the research before they decide whether or not to co-operate.

Permission to carry out an investigation must always be sought at an early stage. As soon as you have an agreed project outline and have read enough to convince yourself that the topic is feasible, it is advisable to make a formal, written approach to the individuals and organizations concerned, outlining your plans. Be honest. If you are carrying out an investigation in connection with a diploma or degree course, say that is what you are doing. If you feel the study will probably yield useful and/or interesting information, make a particular point of that fact — but be careful not to claim more than the investigation merits.

Some LEAs insist that all requests from students wishing to carry out a research project in an LEA institution must be agreed by an LEA officer. In most cases the head of a school or college will have the authority to grant or to refuse access, but clearing official channels is only the first stage in the process. It is an important stage, but you will also need to be quite sure that the people who actually have to give their time to answer your questions or complete your questionnaires are willing to do so. If you are undertaking an investigation in your own institution and know your colleagues well, you may assume everyone will be willing to help. It is unwise to take their co-operation for granted, particularly if any of them have had a bad experience with other researchers.

The experience of one researcher, Stephen Waters, provides interesting insights into some of the problems that can occur, even in a well-prepared study. He had to complete three projects between January and September in connection with an Open University advanced diploma in educational management and decided that, if possible, he would undertake them all in his own school. At the time, he was a scale 2 teacher of English in a comprehensive school and was interested in investigating the role of his own head of department (called director of English). The director expressed interest in and support for the study, and this convinced him that the topic would be worthwhile and would have a good chance of being successfully completed in the time allowed (effectively three months). The preparation proceeded on the following lines:

1. Informal discussion with the head of the school to obtain agreement in principle.
2. Refinement of the topic, statement of the objectives of the study and preparation of a project outline.
3. Discussion with his tutor and further discussion with the director.
4. Minor adjustments made to the project outline and a consideration of the methods to be used.
5. Formal submission of the project outline to the head, together with names of colleagues he wished to interview and certain guarantees and conditions under which the research would be conducted.

The conditions and guarantees were presented as follows:

1. All participants will be offered the opportunity to remain anonymous.
2. All information will be treated with the strictest confidentiality.
3. Interviewees will have the opportunity to verify statements when the research is in draft form.
4. Participants will receive a copy of the final report.
5. The research is to be assessed by the Open University for examination purposes only, but should the question of publication arise at a later date, permission will be sought from the participants.
6. The research will attempt to explore educational management in practice. It is hoped the final report may be of benefit to the school and to those who take part.

So how did it go? This is what he wrote after the project was completed.

> I felt that presenting the guarantees formally was essential. As I was completely inexperienced in research, I had to assure the headmaster that the fieldwork would be carried out with integrity and convince him that he could place his trust in me. Simons' warning was still fresh in my mind, that 'however harmonious relationships in a school appear to be, however democratic the organization, trust does not automatically exist between professionals. It has to be created' (Simons, 1984, p. 127). Moreover, I wished to convince all participants that there was to be, in the words of Preedy and Riches (1985, p. 4) 'some payoff for them in giving access'.

With hindsight, I should have exercised greater caution. Condition 3 could not be met in full since I later found that, although a proper check could be made to verify statements participants had made while being interviewed, there was insufficient time for them to proof-read a full draft. Condition 4 was fulfilled but the cost proved to be prohibitive and I decided to eliminate this condition when the other two case studies were undertaken. This experience certainly alerted me to the danger of promising too much too soon.

It was only when the time drew near for the findings of my research to be disseminated that I became aware of the two areas where the wording of my conditions of research was open to interpretation. The first was that, in promising confidentiality (Condition 2), I had not made it clear what the implications of releasing information would be. As there was insufficient time to release a draft report, no one could check whether my interpretation of what they had said was fair. In any case, as the headmaster was the only person to hold a written copy of my guarantees, the respondents could only interpret the conditions under which they had agreed to participate from my verbal explanation. In retrospect, it would have been better to have provided a duplicated explanation of the course and a written outline of my intentions. Teachers are busy people and it was unreasonable to assume that they would be able to remember a conversation which had taken place dome time before their services were formally required. As it was, whether or not they remembered the guarantees, they were totally dependent on my integrity to present their views in a balanced, objective manner.

More naively, until I was writing the first report, I had not realized that identifying people by role may preserve the guarantee of anonymity for an outside reader, but it did not confer the same degree of obscurity for those within the school. Fortunately, my failure to clarify these matters did not lead to problems — but it could have done.

Stephen Waters learnt a great deal from his first experience of conducting an investigation. He felt he had made some mistakes at his first attempt and was uneasy because he had not been able to fulfil all the conditions and guarantees. He had prepared the ground very well but had not fully appreciated the time and effort involved in reporting back to colleagues and in producing copies of reports. He was concerned at his lack of precision in defining exactly what he meant by anonymity and confidentiality, and made quite sure that in subsequent investigations he clarified the position. He found it harder to know what to do about role conflict. He was a full-time teacher and a part-time researcher — a not unusual combination — and on occasion found it difficult to reconcile the two roles. There were definite advantages in being an 'inside' researcher. For example, he had an intimate knowledge of the context of the research and of the micropolitics of the institution, travel was not a problem and subjects were easily reached. He knew how best to approach individuals and appreciated some of their difficulties. He found that colleagues welcomed the opportunity to air problems and to have their situation analysed by someone who understood the practical day-to-day realities of their task. On the other hand, he found interviewing some colleagues an uncomfortable experience for both parties. As an insider, he quickly came to realize that you have to live with your mistakes after completing the research. The close contact with the institution and colleagues made objectivity difficult to attain and, he felt, gaining confidential knowledge had the potential for affecting his relationship with colleagues. In the event, this did not seem to be the case, but he could foresee situations where problems might have arisen.

When he had successfully completed the diploma course, he was asked whether he felt it had all been worthwhile and whether he had any comments that might be helpful to others who were undertaking a research project for the first time. He wrote as follows:

> I may have given the impression that my research was so fraught with difficulties that it was counter-productive. If so, it is because I wish to encourage the prospective inside-researcher to exercise caution and to be aware of possible pitfalls. In reality, I enjoyed my research immensely and found that the experience of interviewing a cross-section of teaching staff provided me with a much greater working knowledge of the school's management practices. Indeed, my research was so absorbing that at times I found myself struggling to keep pace with my teaching commitments. From Peeke's description, it appears that this problem is not uncommon among teacher-researchers. 'To be a successful researcher can demand a lessening commitment to the task of teacher; it is ironic that a concern for the quality of education may motivate a teacher to involve himself/herself in research, but can also be detrimental to a teacher's own work in the classroom' (Peeke, 1984, p. 24).
>
> I am certain, even without hindsight, that I could have done little to resolve this dilemma. I can honestly say that my research has made me more understanding of the problems confronting those responsible for running the school and has subsequently provoked a great deal of thought about educational issues. If my research had not been practically relevant I would have felt concerned about the extent of my commitment to it. As it was, several recommendations which appeared in my first report have been taken up by the school; my third report on the role of the governing body in the curriculum was placed on the agenda of a governors' meeting in spring and many colleagues have been complimentary about the content of the case studies in general. If I had to choose one strategy that I would encourage prospective inside researchers to adopt, it would be to relate the research report to the pragmatic concerns of the institution. Perhaps, as Vyas (1979) suggests, that is how to overcome the dichotomy between research and practice and the way in which to persuade one's colleagues that participation in research will be as beneficial to them as it is to the researcher.

Whether or not you relate your research to the pragmatic concerns of the institution depends on the nature of your task and your own special concerns, but whether you are an inside or outside researcher, whether you are full time or part time, experienced or inexperienced, care has to be taken to consult, to establish guidelines and to make no promises that cannot be fulfilled. Common sense and courtesy will go a long way to establishing good practice, but remember that research generally takes longer than you think it will, so when you begin the process of negotiating access, look through the following checklist to make sure you have remembered everything and to try to ensure you do not take on more than you can manage.

Negotiating Access Checklist

1. Clear official channels by formally requesting permission to carry out your investigation as soon as you have an agreed project outline.

   Some LEAs insist that requests to carry out research are channelled through the LEA office. Check what is required in your area.

2. Speak to the people who will be asked to co-operate.

   Getting the LEA or head/principal's permission is one thing, but you need to have the support of the people who will be asked to give interviews or complete questionnaires.

3. Submit the project outline to the head/principal, if you are carrying out a study in your or another educational institution.

   List people you would like to interview or to whom you wish to send questionnaires and state conditions under which the study will be conducted.

4. Decide what you mean by anonymity and confidentiality.

   Remember that if you are writing about 'the head of English' and there is only one head of English in the school, the person concerned is immediately recognizable.

5. Decide whether participants will receive a copy of the report and/or see drafts or interview transcripts.

   There are cost and time implications. Think carefully before you make promises.

6. Inform participants what is to be done with the information they provide.

   Your eyes and those of the examiner only? Shown to the head, the LEA etc.?

7. Prepare an outline of intentions and conditions under which the study will be carried out to hand to participants.

   Even if you explain the purpose of the study and the conditions/guarantees, participants may forget.

8. Be honest about the purpose of the study and about the conditions of the research.

   If you say an interview will last ten minutes, you will break faith if it lasts an hour. If you are conducting the investigation as part of a degree or diploma course, say so.

9. Remember that people who agree to help are doing you a favour.

   Make sure you return papers and books in good order and on time. Letters of thanks should be sent, no matter how busy you are.

10. Never assume 'it will be all right'. Negotiating access is an important stage in your investigation.

    If you are an inside researcher, you will have to live with your mistakes, so take care.

A WORD OF WARNING. IF AT SOME TIME IN THE FUTURE, COLLEAGUES OR OTHER RESEARCH WORKERS ASK YOU FOR CO-OPERATION WITH A PROJECT, WOULD YOU BE WILLING TO GIVE THE SAME AMOUNT OF TIME AND EFFORT AS YOU ARE ASKING FOR YOURSELF? IF NOT, PERHAPS YOU ARE ASKING TOO MUCH!

Part II

SELECTING METHODS OF DATA COLLECTION

INTRODUCTION

When you have decided on a topic, refined it and specified objectives, you will be in a position to consider how to collect the evidence you require. The initial question is not 'Which methodology?' but 'What do I need to know and why?'. Only then do you ask 'What is the best way to collect information?' and 'When I have this information, what shall I do with it?'.

No approach depends solely on one method any more than it would exclude a method merely because it is labelled 'quantitative', 'qualitative', 'case study', 'action research', or whatever. As I indicated in Chapter 1, some approaches depend heavily on one type of data-collecting method — but not exclusively. You may consider that a study making use of a questionnaire will inevitably by quantitative, but it may also have qualitative features. Case studies, which are generally considered to be qualitative studies, can combine a wide range of methods, including quantitative techniques. Methods are selected because they will provide the data you require to produce a complete piece of research. Decisions have to be made about which methods are best for particular purposes and then data-collecting instruments must be designed to do the job.

Constraints

The extent of your data-collecting will be influenced by the amount of time you have. This may seem a rather negative approach, but there is no point in producing a grandiose scheme that requires a year and a team of researchers if you are on your own, have no funds and in any case have to hand in the project report in three months.

There are likely to be other constraints. For example, if you wish to observe meetings, you will be limited by the number and timing of meetings that are scheduled to take place in the period of your study. The willingness of people to be interviewed or observed, to complete the questionnaire or diaries will inevitably affect your decisions as to which instruments to use. You may feel that a postal questionnaire would be the most suitable method of obtaining certain information, but postal questionnaires can cost quite a lot of money, so you will have to consider whether funds can be found — and whether this expenditure will be worthwhile.

Reliability and Validity

Whatever procedure for collecting data is selected, it should always be examined critically to assess to what extent it is likely to be reliable and valid. *Reliability* is the extent to which a test or procedure produces similar results under constant conditions on all occasions. A clock which runs ten minutes slow some days and fast on other days is unreliable. A factual question which may produce one type of answer on one occasion but a different answer on another is equally unreliable. Questions which ask for opinions may produce different answers for a whole range of reasons. The respondent may just have seen a television programme which affected opinions or may have had some experience which angered or pleased and so affected response. Wragg (1980:17), writing about interviews, asks: 'Would two interviewers using the schedule or procedure get similar results? Would an interviewer obtain a similar picture using the procedures on different occasions?' These are reasonable questions to put to yourself when you check items on a questionnaire or interview schedule.

There are numbers of devices for checking reliability in scales and tests, such as *test–retest* (administering the same test some time after the first), the *alternate forms method* (where equivalent versions of the same items are given and results correlated) or the *split-half method* (where the items in the test are split into two matched halves and scores then correlated). These methods are not always feasible or necessary, and there are disadvantages and problems associated with all three. Generally, unless your supervisor advises otherwise, such checking mechanisms will not be necessary unless you are attempting to produce a test or scale. The check for reliability will come at the stage of question wording and piloting of the instrument.

Validity is an altogether more complex concept. It tells us whether an item measures or describes what it is supposed to measure or describe. If an item is unreliable, then it must also lack validity, but a reliable item is not necessarily also valid. It could produce the same or similar responses on all occasions, but not be measuring what it is supposed to measure. This seems straightforward enough, but measuring the extent of validity can become extremely involved, and there are many variations and sub-divisions of validity. For the purpose of 100-hour projects that are not concerned with complex testing and measurement, it is rarely necessary to delve deeply into the measurement of validity, though efforts should be made to examine items critically.

Ask yourself whether another researcher using your research instrument would be likely to get the same responses. Tell other people (colleagues, pilot respondents, fellow students) what you are trying to find out or to measure and ask them whether the questions or items you have devised are likely to do the job. This rough-and-ready method will at least remind you of the need to achieve some degree of reliability and validity in question wording, even though it is unlikely to satisfy researchers involved with administering scales and tests with large numbers of subjects. If you wish or need to read further, there are plenty of good texts which should be available in most academic and larger public libraries; for example, Borg (1981:78–92), Moser and

Kalton (1971:353–7), Oppenheim (1966:69–89) and Sapsford and Evans (1984:259–64).

It is often worrying for first-time researchers to know how many questionnaires should be distributed or interviews given. There are no set rules, and you should ask for guidance from your supervisor before you commit yourself to a grand plan that will be far in excess of what is required. Your aim is to obtain as representative a range of responses as possible to enable you to fulfil the objectives of your study and to provide answers to key questions.

Research instruments are selected and devised to enable you to obtain these answers. The instrument is merely the tool to enable you to gather data, and it is important to select the best tool for the job. The following chapters take you through the processes involved in the analysis of documentary evidence, designing and administering questionnaires, planning and conducting interviews, diaries and observation studies. Little attention is given to analysis of data in this part, but all data have to be analysed and interpreted to be of any use, and so Chapters 11 and 12 in Part III should be studied in association with the chapters in Part II.

6

The Analysis of Documentary Evidence

Brendan Duffy

Most educational projects will require the analysis of documentary evidence. In some, it will be used to supplement information obtained by other methods; in others it will be the central or even exclusive method of research. It will be particularly useful when access to the subjects of research is difficult or impossible. This may be frustrating, but documentary analysis of educational files and records can prove to be an extremely valuable source of data (Johnson 1984:23). This chapter aims to explain how to categorize, locate, select and analyse documents. Its approach is derived from historical methods which are essentially concerned with the problems of selection and evaluation of evidence. Such methods have influenced the form of all academic report writing (Barzun and Graff 1977:5).

The Nature of Documentary Evidence

Before beginning the search for documentary evidence, it will be helpful to clarify exactly what kind of document is being used. 'Document' is a general term for 'an impression left by a human being on a physical object' (Travers 1964:2nd edition). Research can involve the analysis of films, videos, slides and other non-written sources, all of which can be classed as documents, but the most common kind of documents in educational research are written as printed sources, so this chapter concentrates on these.

Documents can be divided into primary and secondary sources. *Primary sources* are those which came into existence in the period under research (e.g. the minutes of a school's governors' meetings). *Secondary sources* are interpretations of events of that period based on primary sources (e.g. a history of that school which obtained evidence from the governors' minutes). The distinction is complicated by the fact that some documents are primary from one point of view and secondary from another (Marwick 1970:134). If the author of the school history was the subject of research, for example, his book would become a primary source for the researcher.

Primary sources can in turn be divided into:

(i) *Deliberate sources*, which are produced for the attention of future researchers. These would include autobiographies, memoirs of politicians or educationalists, diaries or letters intended for later publication, and documents of self-justification (Elton 1967:101). They involve a deliberate attempt to preserve evidence for the future, possibly for purposes of self-vindication or reputation enhancement (Lehmann and Mehrens 1971:24).

(ii) *Inadvertent sources*, which are used by the researcher for some purpose other than that for which they were originally intended. They are produced by the processes of local and central government and from the everyday working of the education system. Examples of such primary documents would be the records of legislative bodies, government departments and local authorities; the minutes of academic boards, senior management groups, heads of department meetings and working parties; handbooks and prospectuses; examination papers; attendance registers; personal files; staffing returns; option-choice documents; bulletins; letters and newspapers. Such inadvertent documents are the more common and usually the more valuable kind of primary sources. They were produced for a contemporary practical purpose and would therefore seem to be more straightforward than deliberate sources. This may be the case but great care still needs to be taken with them because it cannot be discounted that inadvertent documents were intended to deceive someone other than the researcher, or that what first appear to be inadvertent sources (some government records, for example) are actually attempts to justify actions to future generations (Elton 1967:102).

A final point about the nature of documents concerns their 'witting' and 'unwitting' evidence. *'Witting'* evidence is the information which the original author of the document wanted to impart. *'Unwitting'* evidence is everything else that can be learned from the document (Marwick 1977:63). If, for example, a government minister made a speech announcing a proposed educational reform, the 'witting' evidence would be everything that was stated in the speech about the proposed change. The 'unwitting' evidence, on the other hand, might come from any underlying assumptions unintentionally revealed by the minister in the language he used, and from the fact that a particular method had been chosen by the government to announce the reform. All documents provide 'unwitting' evidence, but it is the task of the researcher to try to assess its precise significance.

The Location of Documents

Document searches need to be carried out in exactly the same way as literature searches in order to assess whether your proposed project is feasible and to inform yourself about the background to and nature of the subject. The document search may have to cover both national and local sources of evidence.

At the local level, the nature of the project will lead you to particular sources. For example, a project on the relation between a college and its LEA would require a document search in both these institutions and account would have to be taken of their special characteristics. If the college had an academic board, its minutes would be one source; if the LEA had particular sub-committees or working parties which affected the college, their records would be of interest. It can never be assumed, of course, that because documents exist they will be available for research. Some sources may be regarded as too confidential to be released, so enquiries would have to be made about access and availability.

The Selection of Documents

The amount of documentary material that you can study will inevitably be influenced by the amount of time that is available for this stage of your research. It is not usually possible to analyse everything and so you must decide what to select. Familiarity with the different categories of evidence will help you to make decisions about what is fundamental to the project, and 'controlled selection' is then needed to ensure that no significant category is left out (Elton 1967:92). Try not to include too many deliberate sources and take care not to select documents merely on the basis of how well they support your own views or hypotheses. Your aim is to make as balanced a selection as possible, bearing in mind the constraints of time. Periodically, check with your schedule, and if you find you are encroaching on time allocated for the next stage of the research, take steps to reduce your selection. Your perception of what is valuable will grow as the project develops.

The Critical Analysis of Documents

The analysis of documents can be divided into *external* and *internal criticism*, even though these may overlap to a large extent. *External criticism* aims to discover whether a document is both genuine (i.e. not forged) and authentic (i.e. it is what it purports to be and truthfully reports on its subject) (Barzun and Graff 1977:85n). For example, an observer could write a review of a report he had never read. His review would be genuine, because he actually wrote it, but it would not be authentic.

In external criticism it is necessary to know for certain that the author produced the document, so certain questions need to be asked. In the case of a letter, they would include the following:

1. Was the author of a letter known to be in the place from which it came at the time it was written?

2. Do other sources corroborate that the person wrote the letter? Is the letter consistent with all other facts known about the author?
3. Does it use the same arrangements and have the same form as similar documents?
4. Is it typical of other letters or documents written by the author?

It is unlikely you will need or be able to verify any forgeries or hoaxes but an attempt should be made to decide whether a person did actually compose the speech delivered or write the letter with his signature on it.

The method more likely to be used in small-scale educational research projects is *internal criticism*, in which the contents of a document are subjected to rigorous analysis which first seeks answers to the following questions:

1. What kind of document is it? A statute? A policy paper? A set of minutes? A letter from a long correspondence? How many copies are there?
2. What does it actually say? Are the terms used employed in the same way as you would use them? Documents such as statutes or legal papers may employ a specialized language which must be mastered, and private correspondence may use terms in an idiosyncratic way that also needs to be understood (Kitson Clark 1967:64-5).
3. Who produced it? What was its purpose? Did the author aim to inform, command, remind (as in a memorandum) or to have some other effect on the reader? (Travers 1964:120).
4. When and in what circumstances was it produced? How did it come into existence?
5. Is it typical or exceptional of its type?
6. Is it complete? Has it been altered or edited? It may be that there is more chance of completeness if it is published a long time after the events it describes.

After asking these basic questions, you will need to ask further questions about the author:

1. What is known about the author's social background, political views, aims and past experience?
2. Did the author experience or observe what is being described? If so, was he or she an expert on what was being witnessed and a trained observer of the events described?
3. Did the author habitually tell the truth or exaggerate, distort or omit (Travers 1964:119-20)?
4. How long after the event did the author produce the document? Is it possible that memory played tricks?

All these questions may not be relevant to all documents, but in aiming at critical analysis it is important not to accept sources at face value. Examine them carefully. Decide whether a particular political affiliation might possibly influence the tone or emphasis of a paper and try to come to a conclusion based on all the available evidence.

One important aim of critical scholarship is to assess whether fact or bias is the main characteristic of a document (Barzun and Graff 1977:154). Writers will rarely declare their assumptions so it is the task of the researcher to expose them if possible. Watch particularly for any terms that suggest partisanship. Ask yourself whether the evidence supplied in the document convincingly supports the author's arguments. Was the author a supporter of a particular course of action in which he had a stake? If the document goes against the author's own interests, it may increase the likelihood that it tells the truth. Was the author affected by pressure, fear or even vanity when writing the document? (Best 1970:105). Look for clues.

If you detect bias, that does not necessarily mean that the document should be dismissed as worthless. Inferences can still be drawn from the 'unwitting' testimony, even if the 'witting' evidence is thought to be unsound. A prejudiced account of curriculum development, for example, could provide valuable insights into the political processes involved in innovation. The biased document will certainly need to be analysed cautiously and compared with evidence from other sources, but it can still be valuable.

Try to stand in the position of the author of a document and to see the situation through his eyes. Instead of jumping to early conclusions, deliberately seek contrary evidence to test the truthfulness of a document as rigorously as possible — and watch out for your own bias. It may be easier to recognize bias in others than in ourselves, and it is tempting to reject evidence that does not support our case, but try to resist the temptation. The guiding principle in document analysis is that everything should be questioned. Qualities of scepticism as well as empathy need to be developed!

It could be argued that the techniques of document analysis suggested here are merely the application of common sense. This is partly true, but as you study the sources, you will gradually gain insights and detailed knowledge which will give you a 'higher common sense' which will in turn permit a fuller appreciation of the worth of the evidence (Barzun and Graff 1977:130). Eventually, the critical method becomes a habit which will allow you, in Marwick's phrase, to 'squeeze the last drop' from each document (Marwick 1970:138).

7

Designing and Administering Questionnaires

You will only reach the stage of designing a questionnaire after you have done all the preliminary work on planning, consulting and deciding exactly what you need to find out. Only then will you know whether a questionnaire is suitable for the purpose and likely to yield usable data. Ask yourself whether a questionnaire is likely to be a better way of collecting information than interviews or observation, for example. If it is, then you will need to ensure you produce a well-designed questionnaire that will give you the information you need, that will be acceptable to your subjects and which will give you no problems at the analysis and interpretation stage.

It is harder to produce a really good questionnaire than might be imagined. Oppenheim (1966:vii), in the Preface to his book *Questionnaire Design and Attitude Measurement,* wrote that 'the world is full of well meaning people who believe that anyone who can write plain English and has a modicum of common sense can produce a good questionnaire'. He goes on to demonstrate that though common sense and the ability to write plain English will help, that will not be sufficient. Care has to be taken in selecting question type, in question-writing, in the design, piloting, distribution and return of questionnaires. Thought must be given to how responses will be analysed at the design stage, not after all the questionnaires have been returned. Questionnaires are a good way of collecting certain types of information quickly and relatively cheaply as long as subjects are sufficiently literate and as long as the researcher is sufficiently disciplined to abandon questions that are superfluous to the main task.

Exactly What Do You Need to Find Out?

Your preliminary reading and your research plan will have identified important areas for investigation. Go back to your hypothesis or to the objectives and decide which questions you need to ask to achieve those objectives. Then write out possible questions on cards or on separate pieces of paper, to aid ordering at a later stage. You will need several attempts at wording in order to remove ambiguity, to achieve the degree of precision necessary to ensure that subjects understand exactly what you are asking, to check that your language is jargon free, to decide which question type to use and to ensure that you will be able to classify and analyse responses. Guidance about analysis is provided in Chapter 11, and before you complete your questionnaire design you should read this chapter carefully. Time spent on preparation will save many hours of work later on.

Question Type

The more structured a question, the easier it will be to analyse. Youngman (1986) lists seven question types as follows:

VERBAL
or
OPEN
: The expected response is a word, a phrase or an extended comment. Responses to verbal questions can produce useful information but analysis can present problems. Some form of content analysis is required for verbal material (See North *et al.*, 1963, and Krippendorf, 1980) unless the information obtained is to be used for special purposes. For example, you might feel it necessary to give respondents the opportunity to give their own views on the topic being researched — or to raise a grievance. You might wish to use verbal questions as an introduction to a follow-up interview, or in pilot interviews where it is important to know which aspects of the topic are of particular importance to the respondents.

More structured questions will not present so many problems at the analysis stage. Youngman suggests the following:

LIST
: A list of items is offered, any of which may be selected. For example, a question may ask about qualifications and the respondent may have several of the qualifications listed.

CATEGORY
: The response is one only of a given set of categories. For example, if age categories are provided (20–29, 30–39, etc.), the respondent can only fit into one category.

RANKING
: In ranking questions, the respondent is asked to place something in rank order. For example, the respondent might be asked to place qualities or characteristics in order (e.g. punctuality, accuracy, pleasant manner). Number '1' usually indicates the highest priority.

SCALE
: There are various stages of scaling devices (nominal, ordinal, interval, ratio) which may be used in questionnaires, but they require careful handling [see Chapter 11].

QUANTITY   The response is a number (exact or approximate), giving the amount of some characteristic.

GRID   A table or grid is provided to record answers to two or more questions at the same time. For example, *How many years have you taught in the following types of school?*

	1 or 2 years	3 or 4 years	5 or 6 years	more than 6 years
Grammar				
Comprehensive				
Middle				
Independent				
Other (please specify)				

Here, there are two dimensions — type of school and number of years.

Question Wording

Ambiguity, Imprecision and Assumption

Words which have a common meaning to you may mean something different to other people, so you need to consider what your questions might mean to different respondents. For example, suppose you want to find out the extent to which school governors are involved with the school curriculum. You ask:

TO WHAT EXTENT ARE
YOU INVOLVED WITH THE   A great deal   ☐
SCHOOL CURRICULUM?
(Please tick)   A certain amount   ☐

                             Not at all   ☐

What will you do with the responses? What will they mean? 'A great deal' may mean something different for governor A than for governor B. Are you sure you all mean the same thing by 'curriculum'. If you have provided a definition of curriculum for respondents, then you may be able to ask a question of this kind, but not otherwise. When you think about this topic you may decide you have to list specific aspects of the curriculum and specify amounts of time. Ask yourself again exactly what it is you really need to know and then word your question or questions sufficiently precisely to ensure that they mean the same to all respondents.

If respondents are confused, or if they hesitate over an answer, they may pass on to the next question. You want answers to all questions if at all possible, so try to avoid confusion.

The following question seems straightforward, but is it?

WHICH TYPE OF SCHOOL DOES YOUR CHILD ATTEND? (Please tick)	Infant School ☐
	Primary School ☐
	Comprehensive School ☐
	Grammar School ☐
	Other (please specify) ☐

_____

_____

There is an assumption in this question that the respondent has one child. If she has four, one in an infant school, one in a primary school and two in a comprehensive school, what does she do? Does she tick all boxes? Does she put the number of children in the appropriate box? Are you prepared for a category response, or had you intended this to be a list? It may not matter, but if your analysis is planned on the basis of a category response, you will give yourself extra trouble when list responses are given.

Memory

Memory plays tricks. If you were asked to say which television programmes you saw last week, could you remember everything? Could you be sure that one particular programme was last week — or was it the week before? Consider the following question, which appeared in a questionnaire concerned with parents' education. At first sight, it seems perfectly clear.

WHAT SUBJECTS DID YOU STUDY AT SCHOOL?

If respondents left school recently, they may be able to remember quite clearly, but if they left school twenty or more years ago, they may find it difficult to remember. If they do not include English in the list of subjects, would that mean that no English was studied or did they just forget to include it? Consider what information you really need. If you want to know which of a list of subjects that respondent studied, you might decide it would be better to provide a list of subjects which can be ticked. That way, you would ensure that main subjects were covered — but the type of question will depend on the type of information needed.

Knowledge

Take care over questions which ask for information that the respondents may not know or may not have readily to hand. For example, it may seem reasonable to ask a teacher how much capitation is allocated to his or her department. But in many schools, staff have no idea what the sum is. If you need to know, you will also need to consider which members of staff are likely to have that information readily to hand. If respondents have to search for information, they may decide to abandon the entire questionnaire.

Double Questions

It may seem obvious to remind you that double questions should never be asked, but it is easy to overlook the following type of question:

DO YOU ATTEND SWIMMING AND GYMNASTICS CLASSES?

Would the answer 'Yes' mean that you attend both, or one? If you need to know, the question should be divided into:

DO YOU ATTEND SWIMMING CLASSES?
and
DO YOU ATTEND GYMNASTICS CLASSES?

Leading Questions

It is not always easy to spot a leading question, but use of emotive language or the way a question is put can lead respondents to answer questions in one way. For example:

DO YOU NOT AGREE THAT PARENTS SHOULD HAVE THE RIGHT TO HAVE A SAY IN THEIR CHILDREN'S EDUCATION?

It might be difficult for parents to answer 'No' in response to that question.

Presuming Questions

Presuming questions are often a source of error in questionnaires. When they are included it is often because the researcher holds strong views about a subject and overlooks the fact that everyone may not feel the same way. For example:

DOES YOUR EMPLOYER MAKE ADEQUATE PROVISION FOR MATERNITY/PATERNITY LEAVE?

I may think that mothers and/or fathers should be allowed to take leave to care for children from birth to, say, two years. In that case, I might feel that my employer's agreement to allow mothers leave but not fathers is totally inadequate. But what if I think fathers should be allowed no leave? What if I disagree with the whole principle of maternity leave? In that case, the fact that six months leave is allowed for mothers may seem excessive to me. There is a presumption in the question that maternity and paternity leave should be given, and that makes the question invalid.

Hypothetical Questions

Watch for questions that will provide only useless responses. Most hypothetical questions come into this category. For example:

IF YOU HAD NO FAMILY RESPONSIBILITIES AND PLENTY OF MONEY, WHAT WOULD YOU DO WITH YOUR LIFE?

But, a respondent might answer, I do have family responsibilities. I have no money and never shall have as far as I can see, so what's the point of thinking about it?

Offensive Questions and Questions Covering Sensitive Issues

It goes without saying of course that questions that may cause offence should be removed. If you really need information on what might be regarded by some respondents as sensitive issues, you will need to take extra care in the wording and positioning of questions. Some researchers think it is better to place such questions towards the end of the questionnaire, the theory being that if respondents abandon the questionnaire at that point, you at least have answers to all the earlier questions.

Age is often considered to be in the sensitive category and rather than asking respondents to give their exact age, it may be better to ask them to indicate the category, as follows:

WHAT IS YOUR AGE?   20 or younger   ☐

21–24   ☐

25–29   ☐

30–34   ☐

35 or older   ☐

Be careful not to have overlapping categories. It is not uncommon to see age categories listed as 21 or less, 21–25, 25–30, etc.

Appearance and Layout

An excellently prepared questionnaire will lose much if its impact if it looks untidy. Look at some of the published surveys which used a questionnaire as one method of data collection and they will give you ideas about layout. Recipients need to be encouraged to read and to answer the questions and they may be put off by a scruffy document that has been hastily prepared. There are no hard-and-fast rules about layout, but there are a few common-sense guidelines that will help appearance.

1. Questionnaires should be typed (or printed, if you are conducting a very large survey).
2. Instructions should be clear (in capitals, or in different type face).
3. Spacing between questions will help the reader and will also help you when you analyse responses.
4. If you want to keep the questionnaire to a limited number of sheets, it may be better to photo-reduce copy.
5. Keep any response boxes in line towards the right of the sheet. This will make it easy for respondents and will help you to extract information.
6. If you intend to use a computer program, allow space on the right of the sheet for coding.
7. Look critically at your questionnaire and ask yourself what impression it would give if you were the recipient.
8. Take care over the order of the questions. Leave sensitive issues to later in the questionnaire. Start with straightforward, easy-to-complete questions and move on to the more complex topics (writing questions on cards or separate pieces of paper will make it easy to sort and re-sort questions).

Piloting the Questionnaire

All data gathering instruments should be piloted to test how long it takes recipients to complete them, to check that all questions and instructions are clear and to enable you to remove any items which do not yield usable data. There is a temptation in a small study to go straight to the distribution stage, but however pressed for time you are, do your best to give the questionnaire a trial run, even if you have to press-gang members of your family or friends. Ideally, it should be tried out on a group similar to the one that will form the population of your study, but if that is not possible, make do with whoever you can get. Respondents will tell you how long it took to complete the questionnaire, and if they leave any questions unanswered, you will be able to find out why. The purpose of a pilot exercise is to get the bugs out of the instrument so that subjects in your main study will experience no difficulties in completing it and so that you can carry out a preliminary analysis to see whether the wording and format of questions will present any difficulties when the main data are analysed.

Ask your guinea pigs the following questions:

1. How long did it take you to complete?
2. Were the instructions clear?
3. Were any of the questions unclear or ambiguous? If so, will you say which and why?
4. Did you object to answering any of the questions?
5. In your opinion, has any major topic been omitted?
6. Was the layout of the questionnaire clear/attractive?
7. Any comments?

Their responses will enable you to revise the questionnaire ready for the main distribution. It will take you some time to achieve a good standard of design and presentation, but if the preparation is sound, it will save you hours and even weeks of work at the analysis stage.

Distribution and Return of Questionnaires

You will need to make an early decision about how to distribute your questionnaire and what to do about non-response. There are distinct advantages in being able to give questionnaires to subjects personally. You can explain the purpose of the study, and in some cases questionnaires can be completed on the spot. You are likely to get better co-operation if you can establish personal contact, but if that is impossible, you will need to investigate other ways of distribution. Permission can sometimes be obtained to distribute through internal mailing systems. Colleagues and friends may be persuaded to lend a hand and, subject to the head or principal's permission, students may be asked to take questionnaires to parents. If all else fails, you may have to mail copies, but postal surveys are expensive and response rates are generally low, so you would only wish to resort to distribution by post if you found it impossible to contact subjects by any other means.

Unless you are meeting subjects face to face, an accompanying letter will be required, explaining the purpose of the questionnaire, indicating that official approval has been given (if that is the case) and saying what will be done with the information provided. Confidentiality and/or anonymity is usually promised, but before you promise either, decide what that means. Does it mean that there will be no way of identifying respondents or does it mean that only you and specified people will see the returns? Does it mean that you will publish the findings, but that no names will be mentioned in the report? Read again Chapter 5 in which Stephen Waters talks about the problems he encountered over the principle of confidentiality and then decide what you can or cannot promise. It is important to be clear about this before questionnaires are distributed.

Take care with the wording of your letter. A letter that is too brusque or too ingratiating can have an adverse effect on response, so show your draft letter to a few friends and ask their opinion. Remember to give the return date, either in the letter or in a prominent position on the questionnaire. Experience has shown that it is unwise to allow too long. If no date is specified or if too long is given, it becomes too easy for subjects to put the questionnaire to one side, which often means that it will never be seen again. Two weeks is a reasonable time for completion. Give the precise day and date rather than relying on a polite request for the questionnaire to be returned in two weeks' time. For some reason, it seems to help to jog memories if the day as well as the date is stated.

Include a self-addressed envelope (stamped, if respondents have to return the questionnaire by post).

Non-response

Keep a careful record of the date questionnaires were distributed and the date they were returned. Generally, there is a good response at first and then returns slow down. Inevitably, all will not be returned by the specified date, so if you have decided to follow up non-respondents, a second letter and questionnaire will have to be sent.

If you do not ask for names to be given, or devise some system of numbering, you will have no way of knowing who has replied and who has not, and so there can be no follow up. If you promise anonymity, there can be no cunning little symbols that tell you who has replied. Anonymity means that there is no way of linking responses with individuals, so a decision has to be made about follow-up *before* the questionnaires are distributed. As Moser and Kalton (1971:267–8) point out, 'non-response is a problem because of the likelihood — repeatedly confirmed in practice — that people who do not return questionnaires differ from those who do.' Scott (1961), whose article 'Research on Mail Surveys' is a major resource for investigators undertaking large-scale projects involving postal questionnaires, takes the view that if non-response is as low as 10 per cent, in most cases it does not matter very much how biased the non-respondents are, but a higher non-response rate could distort results, and so, if at all possible, some effort should be made to encourage more people to return completed questionnaires.

Opinions vary as to the best time to send out follow-up requests, but in a limited-time project you will need to write about a week after the original date if you are to complete data collection in the time allocated. In some large projects a third and even a fourth reminder will be sent, but the number of returns obtained by this process is unlikely to warrant the time and trouble it will involve.

Analysis of Data

In an ideal world it would be best to wait for all questionnaires to be returned and to glance through all responses before beginning to code and record. In a limited-time project it may be necessary to begin recording responses as soon as the first questionnaires are returned. The procedures for analysing and presenting results, described in Chapter 11, may influence the way you structure the questionnaire and word the questions, so before you decide finally on content and format, read this chapter carefully.

Questionnaire Checklist

1. Decide what you need to know.

List all items about which information is required.

2. Ask yourself why you need this information.

Examine your list and remove any item that is not directly associated with the task.

3. Is a questionnaire the best way of obtaining the information?

Consider alternatives.

4. If so, begin to word questions.

Write questions on separate cards or pieces of paper, to help ordering later on. Consider question type (verbal, grid, etc.).

5. Check wording of each question. Is there any ambiguity, imprecision or assumption? Are you asking respondents to remember? Will they be able to? Are you asking for knowledge respondents may not have? Any double, leading, presuming, hypothetical or offensive questions?

Keep language simple. Don't use words respondents may not understand (that includes technical language), unless you are dealing with a professional group all of whom understand your linguistic short cuts.

6. Decide on the question type.

Verbal, list, category, ranking, scale, quantity or grid. Each type requires a different analysis (see Chapter 11 for further information).

7. When you are satisfied that all questions are well worded and of the right type, sort them into order.

It is often best to leave sensitive issues until later in the questionnaire.

8. Write out instructions to be included on the questionnaire.

Respondents must be quite clear about how they are to answer questions (ticks in boxes, Yes/No, etc.).

9. Consider layout and appearance.

Instructions must be clearly presented (perhaps different typeface? displayed in a prominent position?) Decide whether you need a right-hand margin for coding.

10. Hand over your questionnaire for typing.

Instructions to the typist must be absolutely clear. It is your job to decide how the questionnaire should be displayed, not the typist's.

11. Pilot your questionnaire.

Ideally, it should be sent to people who are similar to your selected sample. However, if that is not possible, ask friends, family or colleagues to help.

12. Try out your methods of analysis. READ CHAPTER 11 BEFORE YOU DECIDE FINALLY ON FORMAT AND ANALYSIS.

Even with five or six completed questionnaires, you will be able to see whether any problems are likely to arise when you analyse the main returns.

13. Make any adjustments to the questionnaire in the light of pilot respondents' comments and your preliminary analysis.

Consider timing. If it took your guinea pigs too long to complete, consider whether any items might be removed.

14. Decide at an early stage how the questionnaires are to be distributed.

By post? Internal mail? By you? If you decide on a postal survey, include a stamped addressed envelope. People are doing you a favour by completing the questionnaire. Don't expect them to pay for the privilege.

15. Unless you are administering the questionnaire personally, include a covering letter and a self-addressed envelope.

Explain the purpose of the study. If you have official approval to carry out the study, say so.

16. Don't forget to say when you would like questionnaires to be returned.

Keep a record of when questionnaires were distributed and when returned.

17. Decide what you are going to do about non-respondents BEFORE you distribute the questionnaires.

Remember you will not be able to send out reminders if all responses are anonymous.

18. Do not distribute questionnaires before checking whether approval is required.

Never assume 'it will be all right'.

19. Begin to record data as soon as completed questionnaires are returned.

You have no time to wait for stragglers.

20. Do not get involved with complicated statistics unless you know what you are doing.

It is perfectly possible to produce a good report without extensive statistical knowledge, as long as the structure of the questionnaire is well thought out.

8

Planning and Conducting Interviews

A major advantage of the interview is its adaptability. A skilful interviewer can follow up ideas, probe responses and investigate motives and feelings, which the questionnaire can never do. The way in which a response is made (the tone of voice, facial expression, hesitation, etc.) can provide information that a written response would conceal. Questionnaire responses have to be taken at face value, but a response in an interview can be developed and clarified.

There are problems of course. Interviews are time-consuming, and so in a 100-hour project you will be able to interview only a relatively small number of people. It is a highly subjective technique and therefore there is always the danger of bias. Analysing responses can present problems, and wording the questions is almost as demanding for interviews as it is for questionnaires. Even so, the interview can yield rich material and can often put flesh on the bones of questionnaire responses.

Moser and Kalton (1971:271) describe the survey interview as 'a conversation between interviewer and respondent with the purpose of eliciting certain information from the respondent'. This, they continue, might appear a straightforward matter, but the attainment of a successful interview is much more complex than this statement might suggest.

Wiseman and Aron (1972) liken interviewing to a fishing expedition and, pursuing this analogy, Cohen (1976:82) adds that 'like fishing, interviewing is an activity requiring careful preparation, much patience, and considerable practice if the eventual reward is to be a worthwhile catch.'

Preparation for interviews follows much the same procedures as for questionnaires. Topics need to be selected, questions devised, methods of analysis considered, a schedule prepared and piloted.

Though question wording is important, it may not be quite as important to be precise about the use of certain terms as for questionnaires, though of course the language you use must be understandable to the respondents. In the chapter on questionnaire design, I gave the example of governors being asked about their involvement in the curriculum and suggested that 'curriculum' might mean something different to different people. In an interview, it would be possible to ask 'To what extent are you involved with the school curriculum?' and then to follow up with a prompt on the lines of 'For example, . . .'

Follow the rules laid down for questionnaire design (no leading, presumptive or offensive questions, etc.). Prepare topics and then questions on cards or on separate pieces of paper, so that you can decide the order of questioning when all topics have been covered. Consider which is likely to be the best order in which to ask questions. The order may be important in establishing an easy relationship with the interviewee. The manner in which you ask questions most certainly will be. Practise interviewing and managing your schedule to make sure your form of questioning is clear, does not antagonize the respondent and allows you to record responses in a way that you can understand when the interview is over.

Type of Interview

Once you have decided what you need to know, a decision will have to be made about the type of interview which is most likely to produce the information required. Grebenik and Moser (1962:16) see the alternative types as ranged somewhere on what they call 'a continuum of formality'. At one extreme is the completely formalized interview where the interviewer behaves as much like a machine as possible. At the other end is the completely informal interview in which the shape is determined by individual respondents. The more standardized the interview, the easier it is to aggregate and quantify the results. A structured interview can take the form of a questionnaire or checklist that is completed by the interviewer rather than by the respondent, and if you are a first-time interviewer, you may find it easier to use a structured format. In the case of the investigation into the involvement of the governors in the school curriculum, you might prepare a schedule on the following lines:

DATE OF INTERVIEW: NAME OF INTERVIEWEE:
VENUE: POSITION:
TOPIC:

(i) To what extent are you involved with the school curriculum?

PROMPT				
	Choice of subject	1	2	3
	Syllabus content	1	2	3
	Allocation of capitation	1	2	3
	Aims and objectives	1	2	3
	Teaching methods	1	2	3

1 = not all all. 2 = to a certain extent. 3 = a great deal. (Provide examples where possible.)

If the interviewee provides information freely, then prompts will not be necessary, but if you particularly wish to know, for example, whether the governor being interviewed has any involvement in establishing the aims and objectives of the school's curriculum, you might need to ask a specific question about that.

The above format allows you to circle responses and if plenty of space is allowed, any interesting comments provided by the interviewee can be jotted down. It saves a great deal of time at the analysis stage and you can be sure all topics are covered. The problem about this format is that you, as the interviewer, decide what questions to ask — and you may not be asking the important questions.

Unstructured interviews centred round a topic may, and in skilled hands do, produce a wealth of valuable data, but such interviews require a great deal of expertise to control and a great deal of time to analyse. Conversation about a topic may be interesting and may produce useful insights into a problem, but it has to be remembered that an interview is more than just an interesting conversation. You need certain information and methods have to be devised to obtain that information if at all possible.

Preliminary interviews can probably be placed at the 'completely unstructured' end of the continuum of formality. This is the stage when you are trying to find out which areas or topics are important and when people directly concerned with the topic are encouraged to talk about what is of central significance to them. At this stage you are looking for clues as to which areas should be explored and which left out. Interviews of this kind require only the minimum of note-taking, and as long as your notes are clear enough to enable you to extract points of interest, and topics for inclusion in the study, they will suffice.

Most interviews carried out in the main data-collecting stage of the research will come somewhere between the completely structured and the completely unstructured point on the continuum. Freedom to allow the respondent to talk about what is of central significance to him or her rather than to the interviewer is clearly important, but some loose structure to ensure all topics which are considered crucial to the study are covered does eliminate some of the problems of entirely unstructured interviews. The guided or focused interview fulfils these requirements. No questionnaire or checklist is used, but a framework is established by selecting topics around which the interview is guided. The respondent is allowed a considerable degree of latitude within the framework. Certain questions are asked, but respondents are given freedom to talk about the topic and give their views in their own time. The interviewer needs to have the skill to ask questions and, if necessary, to probe at the right time, but if the interviewee moves freely from one topic to another, the conversation can flow without interruption.

The advantage of a focused interview is that a framework is

established beforehand and so analysis is greatly simplified. This is important for any research, but particularly so for limited-time studies.

The type of interview selected will to an extent depend on the nature of the topic and what exactly you wish to find out. Preliminary interviews are held to give you ideas about which topics to include in the study, and so an unstructured approach is needed. Where specific information is required, it is generally wise to establish some sort of structure or you may end with a huge amount of information, no time to exploit it and still without the information you need.

Bias

There is always the danger of bias creeping in to interviews, largely because, as Selltiz *et al.* (1951:583) point out, 'interviewers are human beings and not machines', and their manner may have an effect on the respondents. Where a team of interviewers is employed, serious bias may show up in data analysis, but if one researcher conducts a set of interviews, the bias may be consistent and therefore go unnoticed.

Many factors can influence responses, one way or another. Borg draws attention to a few of the problems that may occur:

> Eagerness of the respondent to please the interviewer, a vague antagonism that sometimes arises between interviewer and respondent, or the tendency of the interviewer to seek out the answers that support his preconceived notions are but few of the factors that may contribute to biasing of data obtained from the interview. These factors are called *response effect* by survey researchers.
>
> (Borg 1981:87)

It is easier to acknowledge the fact that bias can creep in than to eliminate it altogether. Gavron, who carried out research into the position and opportunities of young mothers, was very conscious of the dangers inherent in research by solitary interviewers. She wrote, 'It is difficult to see how this [i.e. bias] can be avoided completely, but awareness of the problem plus constant self-control can help' (Gavron 1966:159).

If you know you hold strong views about some aspect of the topic, you need to be particularly careful about the way questions are put. It is even easier to 'lead' in an interview than it is in a questionnaire. The same question put by two people, but with different emphasis and in a different tone of voice, can produce very different responses. Complete objectivity is the aim.

Selecting Interviewees

All researchers are dependent on the good will and availability of subjects, and it is likely to be difficult for an individual researcher working on a small-scale project to achieve a true random sample. If that proves to the be case, you may be forced to interview anyone from the total population who is available and willing at the time. Opportunity samples of this kind are generally acceptable as long as the make-up of the sample is clearly stated and the limitations of such data are realized. However, even in a small study, efforts should be made to select as representative a sample as possible. Say you have 100 subjects and you decide to interview 10 per cent. A random sample will give each of the individuals concerned an equal chance of being selected. You may decide to select every tenth person on an alphabetical list, the first person being selected by sticking a pin in the paper. Everyone selected may not be willing to be interviewed, and so it is wise to have reserve names available. For example, if the twentieth person refused or was not available, you might have decided beforehand, and as part of your research design, to approach the twenty-first.

There may be occasions when you wish to include representative sub-groups. You perhaps wish to interview the appropriate proportion of men and women, of individuals in different age categories or some other sub-group of the target population. If so, you might have the following type of stratification.

TOTAL TARGET POPULATION: 100
Number of men: 60. Number of women: 40.

Instead of selecting every tenth name, the sample population could be selected on the basis of every tenth man and every tenth woman, and so six men and four women would be interviewed.

If you wished to interview men and women who had attended an in-service course, you could take the process one step further, as follows:

	MEN	WOMEN	TOTAL
ATTENDED INSET COURSE	30	10	40
DID NOT ATTEND INSET COURSE	30	30	60
TOTAL	60	40	100

If sex and attendance at the INSET course were particularly important, then the sub-groups would be specified as part of the research design, and the sample would be drawn in the appropriate proportion from each sub-group or cell. This is a rather crude example, but, for a small-scale exercise, will generally be an acceptable way of selecting a sample. If a more scientific approach is required for your project, you will need to read further and to acquire a certain amount of statistical expertise (see Moser and Kalton 1971, Raj 1972, Selkirk 1980, Stuart 1962, Youngman 1984).

Recording and Verification

If you are using a structured format which enables you to tick or circle on a previously prepared questionnaire or checklist, you should leave the interview with a set of responses that can be easily analysed. If you are using a less structured approach, you will need to devise some means of recording responses. Some researchers tape-record interviews (with the respondent's permission) and, if they have ample secretarial support, analyse responses from the transcript. You are unlikely to have such support readily available, and if you have to transcribe yourself, you will have to find something in the region of ten hours for each hour recorded. It is questionable whether you can afford so much time and whether the outcome will be worth the effort. Tape recordings can be useful to check the wording of any statement you might wish to quote and to check that your notes are accurate, but nothing more. With experience, interviewers learn to devise shorthand systems of their own, and as long as notes can be written up immediately, or very soon after the interview ends, it is possible to produce a reasonable record of what was said in the key areas. Careful preparation of an interview guide or schedule will help you to record responses under prepared headings. Prompts listed on the schedule may never be used as prompts, but will serve as sub-headings and will provide some structure for your note-taking.

Whenever possible, interview transcripts, and particularly statements that will be used as direct quotations in the report, should be verified with the respondent. The last thing you want is for a statement to be challenged at the report stage.

Time, Place and Style of the Interview

People who agree to be interviewed deserve some consideration and so you will need to fit in with their plans, however inconvenient it may be for you. Try to fix a venue and a time when you will not be disturbed. Trying to interview when a telephone is constantly ringing and people are knocking at the door will destroy any chance of continuity.

Before you begin to make appointments, make sure official channels, if any, have been cleared. A letter from your supervisor, your head or principal, saying what you are doing and why will always help.

It is difficult to lay down rules for the conduct of an interview. Common sense and normal good manners will, as always, take you a long way, but there are one or two courtesies that should always be observed. You should always introduce yourself and explain the purpose of the research, even if you have an official introductory letter. Make it quite clear what you will do with the information and check whether quotations and views must be anonymous or whether they can be attributed. When you make the appointment, say how long the interview is likely to last and do your best not to exceed the stated time. It is very easy to become so interested in the topic of discussion that time slips by and before you know it, you have exceeded the time limit.

Johnson (1984) makes the point that it is the responsibility of the interviewer, not the interviewee to end an interview. She writes:

> It may have been difficult to negotiate access and to get in in the first place, but the interviewer who, once in, stays until he is thrown out, is working in the style of investigative journalism rather than social research . . . If an interview takes two or three times as long as the interviewer said it would, the respondent, whose other work or social activities have been accordingly delayed, will be irritated in retrospect, however enjoyable the experience may have been at the time. This sort of practice breaks one of the ethics of professional social research, which is that the field should not be left more difficult for subsequent investigators to explore by disenchanting respondents with the whole notion of research participation.
>
> (Johnson 1984:14–15)

Interviewing is not easy and many researchers have found it difficult to strike the balance between complete objectivity and trying to put the interviewee at ease. There are particular difficulties in interviewing senior colleagues, as one first-time researcher found when he interviewed his headmaster. He wrote as follows:

> When interviewing members of the senior staff in the school and, in particular, the headmaster, I was conscious of the degree to which my status as a Scale 2 teacher placed me in a subordinate position, while paradoxically my role as researcher gave me the kind of advantage which Platt (1981) reports is inherent in the interviewer–interviewee relationship. I never managed to relieve the feeling of discomfort which arose from trying to reconcile the two roles. I am certain that the headmaster must have felt a similar internal conflict. It could not have been easy to discuss the school's management process with an inexperienced researcher who was also a member of his own staff. It is to the credit of all the participants that I did not, as far as I can tell, experience anything other than openness and honesty and thereby overcome what might have been a serious limitation to my inside research. Naturally, respondents chose their words carefully as they were aware that colleagues were to be given the opportunity of reading the final report. Diplomacy rather than concealment seemed to be their overriding consideration.

It is difficult to know how these difficulties can be overcome. Honesty about the purpose of the exercise, integrity in the conduct and in the reporting of the interview and a promise to allow interviewees to see the transcript and/or the draft of the report will all help, though cost and time may make it difficult to circulate drafts. Whatever promises are made must be kept, so take care not to promise too much.

A Few Words of Warning

Interviews are very time-consuming. If you allow one hour for the actual interview, there is also travelling time and time lost through any one of numerous mishaps (respondent late home, sudden crisis with children which causes delay, unexpected visitor who interrupts the interview, etc.). Then there is the time needed to consider what has been said during the interview, to go through notes, to extend and clarify points that may have been hastily noted. If you are working full time, you are unlikely to be able to carry out more than one interview in an evening, and even if you are able to devote yourself full time to the task, it is difficult to cope with more than three or four interviews during the course of a day. Your original project plan should take account of the time required for planning and conducting interviews, for coping with cancelled arrangements, second visits and finding replacements for people who drop out.

Interview Checklist

1. Decide what you need to know.	List all the items about which information is required.
2. Ask yourself why you need this information.	Examine your list and remove any item that is not directly associated with the task.
3. Is an interview the best way of obtaining the information?	Consider alternatives.
4. If so, begin to devise questions in outline.	The final form of questions will depend on the type of interview (and *vice versa*).
5. Decide the type of interview.	A structured interview will produce structured responses. Is this what you want, or is a more open approach required?
6. Refine the questions.	Write questions on cards. Check wording (see questionnaire checklist). Decide on question type (verbal, list, category, grid, etc.).
7. Consider how questions will be analysed.	Consult Chapter 11 before deciding finally about question type.
8. Prepare an interview schedule or guide.	Consider the order of questions. Prepare prompts in case the respondent does not provide essential information freely.

9. Pilot your schedule.	Schedules need to be tested, and you need practice in asking questions and recording responses.
10. Revise the schedule, if necessary.	Take account of pilot respondents' comments.
11. Do your best to avoid bias.	If you have strong views about some aspect of the topic, be particularly vigilant. If someone else asked the same question, would they get the same answer?
12. Select who to interview.	Interviews take time. Try to select a representative sample. Decide what to do if selected people are not willing or able to give an interview. Be realistic about the number of interviews that can be conducted in the time available.
13. Try to fix a time and place in which you will not be disturbed.	
14. Make sure official channels have been cleared.	A letter from your supervisor, head or principal, explaining the purpose of the research will be helpful.
15. Introduce yourself, explain the purpose of the research, even if you have a letter.	Say what you intend to do with the information the interviewee gives. Agree anonymity or whether statements can be attributed (see Ch. 5).
16. Say how long the interview will last.	Do your utmost not to exceed the time limit.
17. Try to check the accuracy of your notes with respondents (particularly items to be quoted in the report).	This will take time. Remember to allow for it in your planning. Don't promise to check with respondents if this is likely to prove difficult.
18. Decide whether to tape-record the interview.	Remember it will take a long time to transcribe. Permission must be given. Remember also that if an interview is recorded, it may affect the way a respondent words answers.

19. Honesty and integrity are important.

Make no promises that cannot be fulfilled. Respect respondents' views about anonymity. If you know a respondent has been indiscreet in revealing confidential information, never take advantage.

20. Common sense and good manners will take you a long way.

People who agree to be interviewed are doing you a favour. They deserve some consideration.

21. Don't queer the pitch for other researchers by disenchanting respondents with the whole notion of research participation.

There are any number of ways in which participants can become disenchanted. Appointments not kept or the interviewer arriving late; taking longer than promised; promising to check for accuracy and not doing so; conducting the interview in a hostile manner; failing to thank the respondent.

9

Diaries

On the face of it, diaries are an attractive way of gathering information about the way individuals spend their time. Such diaries are not of course records of engagements or personal journals of thoughts and activities, but records or logs of professional activities. They can provide valuable information about work patterns and activities, provided subjects are clear what they are being asked to do, and why. Completing diary forms is time-consuming, and can be irritating for a busy person who has to keep stopping work to make an entry. If subjects are not fully in sympathy with the task, or have been press-ganged into filling in diary forms, they will probably not complete them thoroughly, if at all. As in all research activities it is essential to meet the people who will be giving up their time, so that you can explain the purpose of the exercise fully, inquire about likely problems and, if possible, resolve them. Reluctant subjects will rarely provide usable data, so preliminary consultation is of the utmost importance.

Oppenheim draws attention to a major problem with this technique:

> that the respondent's interest in filling up the diary will cause him to modify the very behaviour we wish him to record. If, for instance, he is completing a week's diary of his television-viewing behavior, this may cause him to engage in 'duty viewing' in order to 'have something to record', or he may view 'better' types of programs in order to create a more favorable impression.
>
> (Oppenheim 1966: 215).

Diaries generally cover an agreed time-span — a day, a week, a month, or occasionally much longer — depending on what information is required. At certain specified times, 'on the spot' or retrospectively, subjects are asked to say what they did. Diaries deal mainly with behaviour rather than emotions, though they can be adapted to suit whatever purpose you have in mind. Requests for information often take the form of:

'How often in the last hour (day, week, etc.) have you . . .?'
'In the past seven days have you done one of the following? (a), (b), (c), etc.'
'Write down all the things that you did between 4 and 5 o'clock in the afternoon.'

Instructions need to be explicit. Do you really want to know that someone had a cup of tea, paid the milkman or had a bath, or are you only interested in specifically job-related activities?

In any diary exercise there are problems with representativeness. Was this day of the week typical of others or is Monday always the crisis day? Is this week exceptional? As with any other form of data-collecting, some form of check is often desirable.

The Diary Interview Method

As Burgess (1981) notes, diaries can be used as a preliminary to interviewing. Zimmerman and Wieder used them in this way for their ethnographic study of the counter-culture in the USA. In an article on the diary interview method they describe the purpose of diaries:

> Individuals are commissioned by the investigator to maintain . . . a record over some specified period of time according to a set of instructions. The employment of diary materials in this sense, when coupled with an interview (or series of interviews) based on the diary, is also similar to the 'life-history' method . . . The technique we describe emphasizes the role of diaries as an observational log maintained by subjects which can then be used as a basis for intensive interviewing.
>
> (Zimmerman and Wieder 1977: 481)

So Zimmerman and Wieder see a use for diaries as a preliminary for interviewing in cases where it may not at first be clear what are the right questions to ask, and

> the diarist's statement is used as a way of generating questions for the subsequent diary interview. The diary interview converts the diary — a source of data in its own right — into a question-generating and, hence, data-generating device.
>
> (p. 489)

The potential for diaries as question-generating devices is clear, but Zimmerman and Wieder take this process a step further. They view the use of a diary, in conjunction with the diary interview, as an approximation to the method of participant observation. They point to some of the difficulties of participant observation, including: the length of time involved; the fact that any observer, even a participant, may have an effect on normal behaviour; and, in some studies, moral, legal or ethical constraints. They propose the use of the diary interview method 'for those situations where the problems of direct observation resist solution, or where further or more extended observation strains available resources' (p. 481).

They asked their subjects to record in chronological order the activities in which they engaged over a seven-day period, following the formula what/when/where/how?

The 'What?' involved a description of the activity or discussion recorded in the diarists' own categories. 'When?' involved reference to the time and timing of the activity, with special attention to recording the actual sequence of events. 'Where?' involved a designation of the location of the activity, suitably coded to prevent identification of individuals or places. The 'How?' involved a description of whatever logistics were entailed by the activity.

(p. 486)

Clearly, diarists must be of a certain educational level to understand the instructions, let alone complete the diary. They must also have time. If you are asking colleagues to co-operate by completing diaries, be very sure that the diary is the best way of obtaining the information you need and that you can convince your subjects that what they are doing is likely to be of practical use.

A less wide-ranging approach was adopted by Bradley and Eggleston (1976) in their study of probationer teachers in three LEAs. Probationer teachers were asked to keep weekly diaries on three separate occasions during the term, and a form similar to that used by Hilsum and Cane (1971) in their research *The Teacher's Day* was adopted. This asked for information about professional activities in which teachers might have engaged, outside scheduled teaching time. One form, an example of which is given in Figure 9.1, was provided for each day of the week, including the weekend.

In addition to keeping the weekly diaries, the probationer teachers were asked to make a note of things to which they gave a lot of thought during the day (e.g. problems of non-readers, keeping noise to an acceptable level), to make a list of people with whom they had discussed matters relating to their work and to indicate what they had done in any periods when they were released from teaching.

The type of questions will, of course, reflect the emphasis of the study. Completed diaries can provide a wealth of information, and this can be a problem in itself unless the same care is taken in wording the questions as is necessary for questionnaires and interviews, and unless thought has been given as to how the information will be analysed, *before* the diaries are designed and completed.

The Critical-Incidents and Problem-Portfolio Approaches

One way of investigating the work people do is to ask them to describe what 'critical incidents' occurred over a specified period of time (Flanagan 1951, 1954). Writing about the problems facing heads of department in further education, Oxtoby asks how heads of department can attempt to find out how their time is spent, and how they can sift the key aspects of their job from the trivial ones:

Analysing work activities can be approached from many different points of view . . . Some methods are not capable of being used by HoDs to monitor their own activities, for example, interviews, observation and activity sampling, questionnaires and checklists. More appropriate methods are those which rely on written activity records of one kind or another, such as diaries, critical incident reports, problem portfolios. The use of a job diary is perhaps the most simple and widely accepted way of finding out how time is spent. But self-recording can be inaccurate — many of the shorter episodes tend to get omitted — and compiling a detailed diary is usually a tiresome and onerous business. Although it is undoubtedly valuable in terms of enabling people to make more effective use of their time, a diary does not provide much reliable information about the skills or qualities developed. Moreover, the prospect of using diaries to compare differences between large numbers of staff and their jobs is extremely daunting, if only because of the difficulties involved in handling the data. There are snags, therefore, in employing job diaries to analyse the diversity of HoD activities.

The critical incident technique is an attempt to identify the more 'noteworthy' aspects of job behaviour and is based on the assumption that jobs are composed of critical and non-critical tasks. For example, a critical task might be defined as one which makes the difference between success and failure in carrying out important parts of the job. The idea is to collect reports as to what people do that is particularly effective in contributing to good performance and then to scale the incidents in order of difficulty, frequency and importance to the job as a whole. The technique scores over the use of diaries in that it is centred on specific happenings and on what is judged to be effective behaviour. But it is still laborious and does not lend itself to objective quantification.

An even more flexible and productive approach for colleges and HoDs is possibly that due to Marples (1967), who suggests that one measure of a manager's ability may be expressed in terms of the number and duration of 'issues' or *problems* being tackled at any one time. He advocates the compilation of 'problem portfolios', recording information about how each problem arose, methods used to solve it, difficulties encountered and so on. Such an analysis also raises questions about the job incumbent's use of time: what proportion of his time is occupied in checking; in handling problems given to him by others; on self-generated problems; on 'top priority' problems; on minor issues?

(Oxtoby 1979: 239–40)

In his study, Oxtoby sent a questionnaire to 240 heads of department in colleges of further education in England and Wales, asking them 'What was the most difficult task or situation with which you had to deal during the past two or three days?' Another way of approaching the task would have been to ask heads of department to complete a diary over a period of one week, asking them to describe in about ten lines the most difficult problem or situation they had to deal with each day, why it arose, why it was difficult and how they acted.

In a 100-hour project, you are unlikely to survey 240 departments, but you may wish to study work activities in your institution; and, if so,

Activity	Time worked during school's normal teaching hours but outside your scheduled teaching time		Time worked outside school's normal teaching hours		Friday
	in school	*out of school*	*in school*	*out of school*	
	minutes	minutes	minutes	minutes	
Marking and assessing, e.g. marking exercise books, exams, tests					
Writing reports for head, parents, probation officer, other schools; making assessments for school record cards, reports					
Lesson planning, e.g. referring to textbooks, taking notes; estimating equipment required; writing, referring to record/forecast of work					
Making equipment					
Staff meeting					
Staff duties, e.g. attending PTA, professional association, school sports					
Special occasion, e.g. Open Day, Sports Day, Speech Day, jumble sale, school social occasion, school concert, play					
Professional course, attending course or conference on professional matters					

Activity							
Reading for background information, e.g. professional journals							
Club activities, e.g. attending, organizing football, netball fixture (home/away); games practice, chess, orchestra, drama							
Administration, e.g. (excluding club activities) estimating stock requirements; planning timetable; planning, organizing school outing; making duty roster							
Recording, e.g. copying, calling out list of names, marks; counting money; copying information into reports or records; totalling registers							
Using equipment, e.g. giving out, collecting equipment (incl. books); tidying; clearing up desks, room; searching for equipment							
Pupil welfare, e.g. speaking to parents, pupil(s) about home, personal interests; dealing with pupils' private property; dealing with pupil(s) who is/are unwell							
Direct tuition, e.g. instructing, demonstrating; marking with pupil; listening to, watching (with class) radio, TV, visiting speaker							
Supervision/patrol; e.g. patrolling building, playground; coach escort; detention: (a) when on duty, (b) when not on duty							

Figure 9.1 A diary form (adapted from Bradley and Eggleston 1976).

critical-incidents or problem-portfolio techniques may be appropriate. They have the advantage of not requiring your subjects to spend substantial amounts of time completing a diary with what may seem rather trivial items, and they allow you to see what the subjects themselves considered to be problems.

As will be apparent from the above, there are problems in the use of diaries as a method of gathering evidence, not least the time needed to complete the forms. However, diaries can produce a wealth of interesting data and are relatively simple to administer. Analysis of completed forms is not so simple however, so you will need to consider how responses will be coded before you put your subjects to the trouble of filling in the diaries. If you are using diaries as part of a project, you may wish to consult the checklist below before you distribute them.

Diaries and critical-incidents checklist

1. Before you decide to use diaries ask yourself:
    What information do I need?
    Do I really need this information?
    If 'yes', then is this the best way of getting hold of it?
    If 'no', think again.
2. Diary completion is quite a sophisticated task, so diaries are not generally suitable tools to use with people who have a limited educational background.
3. You will need to take the same care over wording the questions as in questionnaires and interviews.
4. Subjects will not be willing to complete diaries for more than a limited period of time, so decide what the time-scale is to be (one week, one day, one hour?). Then ask yourself whether you can get sufficient information to make the exercise worthwhile.
5. You are unlikely to get co-operation (and so usable data) unless subjects know *why* they are being asked to carry out this chore, *how* they are to do it, *what* will be done with the information and *when* it has to be done.
6. Thus, you must spend time at the planning stage discussing with your subject(s) what is involved.
7. As in all data collection, decide how you propose to deal with responses *before* you ask for diaries to be completed, or you may end up with a pile of responses that do not fall into any sort of pattern. You may decide after the event that it would have been better to design the diary form in a different way. It is too late after the event.
8. It may help, if you can find the time, to check progress. If you are asking people to carry out this task for more than one day, evidence seems to indicate that a solicitous enquiry about how things are going may help them to keep on with the task.

9. Your subjects are doing you a favour by completing the diary. They may be willing to spend time because they want to help you, because they think the exercise is worthwhile, or because they did not like to say 'no'. Whatever their motive, they deserve your thanks and, if possible, feedback about results.

10. Remember to get permission to carry out a diary exercise, from the head of your institution *and* from the people you will be asking to complete the diaries. Do not assume 'it will be all right'.

10

Observation Studies

The teacher researcher, or the student working on his own, is at no disadvantage compared to the research team when he is working personally on observation and analysis of individual instances. Observation, however, is not a 'natural' gift but a highly skilled activity for which an extensive background knowledge and understanding is required, and also a capacity for original thinking and the ability to spot significant events. It is certainly not an easy option.

(Nisbet 1977:15)

Anyone who has carried out an observation study will no doubt agree with Nisbet that observation is not an easy option. Careful planning and piloting are essential, and it takes practice to get the most out of this technique. However, once mastered, it is a technique that can often reveal characteristics of groups or individuals which would have been impossible to discover by other means. Interviews, as Nisbet and Watt (1980:13) point out, provide important data, but they reveal only how people *perceive* what happens, not what actually happens. Direct observation may be more reliable than what people say in many instances.

A major difficulty for anyone who both observes and participates in a process is that familiarity with the environment and with the characteristics of colleagues who are being observed may affect objectivity. A non-participant observer will always attempt to distance himself or herself from the group being observed, as happens when a researcher sits in a meeting room and notes whatever behaviour or activities are the subject of the research. Zimmerman and Wieder (1977) describe the non-participant observer as a sort of spectral presence. Participant observers are certainly not spectral. They actually take part in some or all of the activities that are to be observed. For example, members of a school staff might take the role of participant observer in their school, or a researcher might move into an environment for a period of time and attempt to become immersed in the life of the community.

Lacey (1976:65) defined participant observation as 'the transfer of the whole person into an imaginative and emotional experience in which the fieldworker learned to live in and understand the new world'. He was writing about his experiences at 'Hightown Grammar' where, for three years, he taught, observed classes and talked to teachers and pupils. He describes his methodology in *The Organisation and Impact of Social Research*. Studies of this kind are well beyond the scope of what you will be asked to do in small projects, but the problems of participant observation are similar, whatever the size of the undertaking. Researchers who spend long periods in the company of the group they are studying, and who try to participate fully in the lives of those who are being studied, run the risk of being unable to see other points of view. If you are researching in your own institution, you will be very familiar with the personalities, strengths and weaknesses of colleagues, and this familiarity may cause you to overlook aspects of behaviour that would be immediately apparent to a non-participant observer seeing the situation for the first time. However, whether you are observing as a participant or a non-participant, your role is to observe and record in as objective a way as possible, and then to analyse and to interpret the data you gather.

Recording and Analysing

There are numbers of ways of recording what happens in the classroom or at a meeting, but before a method can be selected a decision has to be made about exactly what is to be observed. This is harder than might at first appear. It is impossible to record everything, so you need to be clear whether you are interested in the *content* or *process* of a lesson or meeting, in *interaction* between individuals, in the *nature of contributions* by teacher, pupil or committee members, or in *some specific aspect* such as the effectiveness of questioning techniques. Once you have decided what you wish to find out and have satisfied yourself that you need this information to further your research, then you will be in a position to consider what methods of recording the data will best suit your purposes.

Video and Audio Recording

In a well-financed project with a team of researchers, it may be possible to record or even to film what is happening in a class or meeting room. However, as with interviews, in a small project there is unlikely to be the money or the time to deal with audio recordings or video tapes. Other methods have to be found which will enable you to record on the spot in an orderly way so that after the event, analysis is quick and easy.

Interaction-Process Analysis

There are many published observation schedules and accounts of different methods of observing individuals and groups in different contexts (Flanders 1970, Simon and Boyer 1975, Wragg and Kerry

1978, Galton 1978, Cohen 1976, Hopkins 1985, Williams 1984), several of which are based on a system of interaction-process analysis devised by R.F. Bales (1950). Bales's system attempted to describe the behaviour of individuals in groups. He devised a method of classifying or coding, which enabled the observer to record under one of twelve headings which he considered were sufficiently comprehensive to classify different types of behaviour likely to occur in any group. Examples of his categories of behaviour are 'shows tension release' (jokes, laughs, shows satisfaction) and 'shows antagonism' (deflates others' status, defends or asserts self).

Since 1950 many different types of categories have been devised, some relatively simple and others extremely complicated. The Flanders system, which was derived from the Bales method of classifying behaviour, is one of the best known. Flanders (1970) devised ten categories of teacher/student behaviour (the Flanders interaction-analysis categories), which the observer used as a basis for categorizing and recording what took place in the classroom. Observers were required to record what was happening every three seconds and to enter the appropriate category number on a prepared chart. The problem about Flanders-type systems is that the categories are quite complex, have numbers of sub-sections and inevitably involve the observer making some value judgements as to which category is closest to particular types of observed behaviour.

The requirement to record every three seconds means that the observer has to be fully conversant with categories and criteria and to recall instantly the number assigned to particular aspects of behaviour. This takes a considerable amount of practice. The more complicated (and so more thorough) the system of categories, the harder it is to manage.

Open University course D101 (now replaced) proposed a much simpler system, though based on similar principles to Bales/Flanders. Students were asked to observe two meetings on an Open University television programme, making use of an abbreviated system devised originally to study management skills and behaviour by the Huthwaite Research Group. Six categories were proposed to help students to classify behaviour in meetings, as follows:

1. PROPOSING	A behaviour which puts forward a new concept, suggestion or course of action.
2. SUPPORTING	A behaviour which involves a conscious and direct declaration of support or agreement with another person or his concepts.
3. DISAGREEING	A behaviour which involves a conscious and direct declaration of difference of opinion, or criticism of another person's concepts.
4. GIVING INFORMATION	A behaviour which offers facts, opinions or clarification to other individuals.

| 5. SEEKING INFORMATION | A behaviour which seeks facts, opinions or clarification from another individual or individuals. |
| 6. BUILDING | A behaviour which extends or develops a proposal which has been made by another person. |

These categories describe the kind or style of behaviour engaged in, not the content of what is being said. If you think back to a meeting you have recently attended, you may already envisage difficulties in sorting out one category from another. Several different categories can sometimes be identified within one sentence. A disagreeing statement may also propose, and a supporting statement may also give information. It could be argued that many statements could be categorized as either giving or seeking information. Managing systems of this kind requires practice and careful consideration beforehand about how certain behaviour will be classified, but once the technique has been mastered, it can produce useful data about the behaviour of individuals in groups.

The way in which observations are recorded is largely a matter of personal preference. Using the above categories of behaviour, entries could be made on a table plan, as in Figure 10.1. Numerical entries are made in the appropriate box (e.g. '1' for Proposing, '2' for Supporting, etc.), and the total number of entries listed in whichever format seems most suitable. One way would be to prepare a chart, as shown in Figure 10.2.

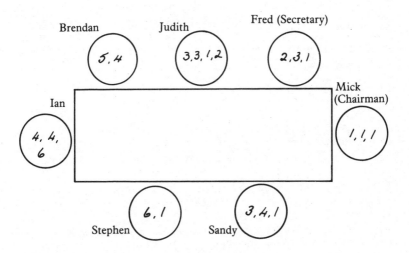

Figure 10.1 Table plan recording individual behaviour according to categories.

Participants Categories

	1	2	3	4	5	6	Totals
Chairman (Mick)	✓✓✓						③
Secretary (Fred)	✓	✓	✓				③
Judith	✓	✓	✓✓				④
Brendan				✓	✓		②
Ian				✓✓		✓	③
Stephen	✓					✓	②
Sandy	✓		✓	✓			③
Totals	⑦	②	④	④	①	②	

Figure 10.2 Chart recording total number of entries for each behaviour category.

Contributions could be plotted on a graph or presented in whichever way illustrated the nature of the contributions made. It would not of course be enough merely to present the information as observed. Commentary on the significance (or lack of significance) would be necessary and inferences might be drawn about the nature of individual contributions.

Content and Interventions

The analysis of the content of a lesson or of a meeting, or consideration of the topics covered, is rather more straightforward. If you were observing a governors' meeting, you might devise a chart as shown in Figure 10.3.

If the main interest was in who made most contributions and spent most time speaking, then a simple chart on the lines shown in Figure 10.4 might be devised. A vertical line would indicate that that person spoke for a set time (say half a minute) or less. A following horizontal line would indicate that the same person continued to speak for the same set period.

MEETING: Governors of Bramhope High School

DATE: 1.12.86

TIME: 6.30–8.30 p.m.

	APPROX. TIME SPENT (in minutes) OR NUMBER OF TIMES TOPICS WERE MENTIONED	PERCENTAGE OF TOTAL RECORDED
ADMINISTRATION (Minutes, letters etc.)		
RESOURCES		
STAFFING (Appointment of new Scale I teacher of English)		
DISCIPLINE		
PTA		
CURRICULUM		
OTHER (Sports Day, Caretaker's illness, etc.)		

Figure 10.3 Example of a chart for recording the content of a governors' meeting.

Participants	
Mick	/// =
Fred	
Judith	/ ≡ //
Brendan	//
Ian	//// = / ≡
Stephen	//
Sandy	/ = //
Multiple speaking	///

Figure 10.4   Example of a chart recording speaking contributions by individuals.

The two previous examples are simple to manage and produce useful, though limited information. If all you need to know is who spoke most or which topics took up most time, then they will suffice, and adaptations of these charts have been used to good effect in many different situations. However, if you wish to find out who says most about what, then a more complex system is needed, and it may be best to make fuller notes during the course of the meeting or the class and then to transfer to a summary chart.

There are a number of ways in which such on-the-spot records can be kept. Shaw (1978:10) suggests that sheets of lined paper should be prepared, marked so that each line represents one minute. The starting time and the topic is entered in a wide vertical margin and every time someone speaks, his or her initials are entered in the margin. A note of the contribution made is entered on the sheet and a line drawn after each topic. Notes are then entered on a summary sheet, as illustrated below. This method may not suit you but you need to try out one or two different methods to see which you find easy for recording and for analysis and interpretation after the event.

School: Bramhope High
Meeting: Governors
Date: 1.12.86

	Admin. (Minutes, etc.)	Curriculum (general)	Curriculum (resources)	Exams	New appointment	PTA	Discipline	Other	No.	%
Chairman (Industrialist)	HHT HHT			HHT //		/	HHT //	///	28	22.6
Secretary (ILEA official)	HHT HHT							//	12	9.7
Mrs A (Parent governor)						//	///		5	4.0
Mrs B (Parent governor)									0	0
Mr C (Councillor)					/		HHT	//	8	6.5
Mr D (Councillor)					///		//		5	4.0
Mr E (Bank manager)					/		/		2	1.6
Dr F (LEA adviser)	HHT			//	////		/		12	9.7
Mrs G (Staff representative)					////	/	////		9	7.2
Miss H (sixth-form representative)									0	0
Head	///	HHT /		HHT	///		HHT HHT	//	29	23.4
Deputy head	//	///				//	HHT //		14	11.3
Total time (in minutes)	30	9	0	14	16	6	40	9	124	100

Figure 10.5 Content and interventions chart.

It can be seen from the content and interventions chart (Fig. 10.5) that the chairman and the head spoke more often than anyone else and two governors remained silent throughout. Apart from the head's report, practically no time was spent on curricular matters. The agenda item which took most time and caused greatest controversy was the discipline item. The head asked for the governors' agreement to the suspension of a fourth-form boy whose behaviour had been so outrageous that his presence in school not only prevented other pupils from learning but also constituted a danger to individuals and to the fabric of the building. Not all members of the committee participated, but those who did had strong feelings.

Interactions

The interventions chart is not able to show who talks to whom, and if this information is required, something on the lines shown in Figure 10.6 will be required. The idea is that a seat plan is prepared beforehand and when committee members or students are seated, their names are entered. Communication between individuals is indicated by an arrow and then by additional arrow heads. Ticks next to individuals' names indicate communication to the whole group. 'M' indicates multiple speaking.

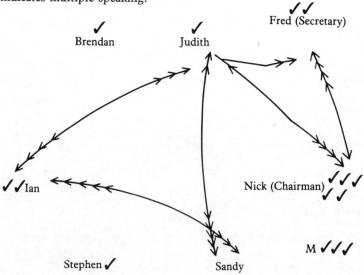

✓ = Communication to the whole group
M = Multiple speaking

Figure 10.6 Interaction chart.

This type of charting can provide indications of who generally interacts with whom. It can indicate pairings and suggest further areas for investigation. For instance, if the head spends most of his time talking to the LEA adviser, does that indicate that he sees the adviser as the most important member of the committee and so must be the main focus for his attention? It is dangerous to jump to conclusions without more evidence than an interaction chart can provide, but such a chart does at least provide clues about relationships, and opens up areas for further investigation.

Selecting a Method

Simon and Boyer (1975), Flanders (1970), Wragg and Kerry (1978), Galton (1978), Cohen (1976), Williams (1984) and Hopkins (1985) provide many examples of charts, grids, categories and methods of recording which will give you a range of useful ideas for devising schemes of your own. The sad fact is that in spite of all the tried-and-tested methods that have been employed by experienced researchers over the years, there never seems to be an example that is quite right for the particular task. Inevitably, you will find you have to adapt or to devise a completely new approach, and all new systems need careful piloting and refining in the light of experience. If you have access to only one class or one meeting, you must be quite sure that your selected method of recording is going to work. You will probably need to invent your own system of shorthand symbols and these will have to be memorized. You will need to decide how often to record what is happening (all the time? every three seconds? every five minutes? every twenty minutes?) and with whom (all the class? a selected group?) Preparation is all-important. Charts and seating plans have to be prepared. You will need to discuss with the teacher or the chairman of the committee where it would be best to sit. Opinions vary. In a classroom there is some merit in sitting where the pupils can see you. At least that way they are not always turning round to see what you are doing, but if the teacher has other views, listen. An observer can never pass entirely unnoticed, but the aim is to be as unobtrusive as possible so that observed behaviour is as close to normal as possible.

Preparation

At the beginning of this chapter, I said that observation can often reveal characteristics of groups or individuals that would have been impossible to discover by other means. This has been demonstrated in many research studies which made extensive use of observation techniques, but the greatest care has to be taken to ensure that you get the most out of the periods of observation. You will not have three years in which to begin an investigation with an entirely open mind and to evolve hypotheses and methods as you go along. It is likely you will have one opportunity only to observe a meeting or a class and so you will need to be quite clear about the purpose of your observation and why you are observing that particular group or individual. You may discover that unforeseen and interesting information emerges during the course of your observation, but you will be mainly dependent on the decisions taken before you begin your period of observation for the type of data you eventually gather. If you make a decision before a meeting that your main interest is the content of the meeting, then charts, grids or checklists have to be devised with that aim in mind. It will be too late to record interactions. If your main interest is process, then other methods will have to be found to record how a lesson or a meeting is conducted. As you select and refine your methods, keep constantly in mind the questions 'What do I need to know?' 'Why do I need to know it?' and 'What shall I do with this information when I have it?' Pilot exercises and practice in recording will answer some of these questions and will point to weaknesses in technique. When you begin your one-off observation exercise, you need to be as sure as you can that you are prepared and ready.

After the Event

The task is not complete when the observation has taken place and records have been made. If you were observing a governors' meeting and felt at the end of it that it was rather ineffectual, you would need to analyse the reasons. Was the process altogether too formal? Did the chair speak for 80 per cent of the time and the head the remaining 20 per cent? Were contributions from parent governors dismissed? Some forms of interaction analysis can help you to classify process and content, but whatever methods of recording you have selected, it is essential to consider the event as a whole, as soon after the event as you can. Review in your mind what took place and decide whether any conclusions can be drawn that might be of interest in your study.

Useful though grids, forms and checklists are, they cannot take account of emotions, tensions and hidden agendas. Shaw (1975) in his study of change at St Luke's College of Education used a chart to record interventions in an academic board meeting, but he recognized the limitations of this technique. His subsequent account of the manoeuvring and the lobbying, the anxieties, the delaying tactics and the influence of certain key members of the institution indicates very clearly the importance of the micropolitical processes at work in any organization, the effect they can have on the way meetings are conducted and decisions reached.

If you observe a meeting or a class as part of your investigation, make efforts to place what you see in its organizational and/or curricular context, to look beyond the event itself and, in Nisbet's words, 'to spot significant events'.

Observation Studies Checklist

1. Decide exactly what you need to know.

   List all topics/aspects about which information is required.

2. Consider why you need this information.

   Examine your list and remove any item that is not directly associated with the task.

3. Is observation the best way of obtaining the information you need?

   Consider alternatives.

4. Decide which aspects of the lesson/meeting/event you need to investigate.

   Are you particularly interested in content, process, interaction, intervention — or something else?

5. Request permission.

   Clear official channels and also discuss what is involved with individuals concerned (e.g. the teacher, chairman, etc.)

6. Devise a suitable grid, checklist or chart.

   Consult published examples and adapt where necessary.

7. Consider what you will do with the information.

   Is it likely to produce anything of interest? Will the data be sufficiently complete to enable you to come to any conclusions?

8. Pilot your method and revise if necessary.

   Memorize categories. Devise your own system of shorthand (symbols, letters, etc.). Practise recording until you are confident you can cope.

9. Prepare carefully before the observation.

   Draw a plan of the room, indicating seating arrangements and layout. Make sure you have enough copies of grids or checklists. Consult minutes of previous meetings, agenda, scheme of work, etc.

10. Discuss where you will sit with the teacher or chairman and agree how you are to be introduced.

    You want to be as unobtrusive as possible. Exactly where you sit will depend on your own preferences and the views of participants.

11. Remember that no grid, however sophisticated, will tell the full story.

Try to place the event in its organizational/curricular context.

12. Analyse and interpret the data.

Factual statements about what has been observed are only part of the task. Consider what the facts indicate or infer.

13. Don't forget to thank the people who have allowed you to observe.

You may need their help again!

Part III

ANALYSING EVIDENCE AND PRESENTING THE FINDINGS

INTRODUCTION

Data collected by means of questionnaires, interviews, diaries or any other method mean very little until they are analysed and assessed. Earlier chapters have stressed the need to consider how responses will be analysed at the planning and design stage. Gathering large amounts of information in the hope that something will emerge is not to be recommended in any investigation, but particularly not for researchers who have as little as 100 hours in which to complete a study. As I said in the Introduction at the beginning of this book, those of you who have a limited statistical background cannot attempt highly complex surveys involving advanced statistical techniques, but that does not mean that a worthwhile study cannot be carried out. It is all a case of working within your limitations and selecting research methods which are suitable for the task and which can be readily analysed, interpreted and presented.

Before you begin your study of the next two chapters there are a number of issues which have been raised earlier but which need to be reiterated. In Chapter 1, I briefly discussed the question of generalization. Bassey (1981:85–6) drew attention to the problems of generalizing from insufficient data, and made a strong case for individual researchers working to a limited time scale to produce research structured in response to an existing or potential problem so that the results might be of use to the institution. Such research, he felt, might go some way to solving a particular problem or lead to informed discussion of how a particular problem might be tackled. He commended the descriptive and evaluative study of single pedagogic events and (writing about case study methods), concluded that

> an important criterion for judging the merit of a case study is the extent to which the details are sufficient and appropriate for a teacher working in a similar situation to relate his decision-making to that described in the case study. The relatability of a case study is more important than its generalizability.
>
> (Bassey 1981:85)

I raise this issue again here because in the analysis, interpretation and presentation of data, care has to be taken not to claim more for results than is warranted, and equal care has to be taken not to attempt generalizations based on insufficient data. In a 100-hour project, generalization is unlikely, but relatability may be entirely possible. Well-prepared, small-scale studies may inform, illuminate and provide a basis for policy decisions within the institution. As such, they can be invaluable. There is no need to apologize about inability to generalize, but there would be every need to apologize if data were manipulated in an attempt to prove more than could reasonably be claimed.

11

Analysis and Presentation of Information

Sandy Goulding

In undertaking any small-scale investigation or large-scale study, the researcher must be able to understand the methods by which the information or data collected may be analysed and presented; the same methods may be used to present data culled from official sources. It is, however, likely that the size of small-scale studies will be such that the results produced will be illuminative rather than generalizable.

There are two broad categories into which statistical methods fall: descriptive and inferential. Descriptive statistical methods provide 'pictures' of the group under investigation: these 'pictures' may be in the form of charts, tables, percentages, averages and so on. Inferential statistical methods have a quite different purpose; they may involve the use of descriptive statistics, but their prime aim is to draw implications from the data with regard to a theory, model or body of knowledge.

The methods most likely to be useful in analysing information gained from investigations of a limited nature are those of descriptive statistics. Whether the information arises from questionnaires which respondents themselves complete, or whether it arises from a structured interview situation where the interviewer completes a schedule, makes no difference to the way that the data can be handled. The purpose, therefore, of this chapter is to explain some of the descriptive methods which are useful in analysing and presenting data derived from small-scale surveys using questionnaires or structured interview schedules.

No special statistical knowledge is required to understand and to make use of these methods. One straightforward way of recording data is described; the use of different kinds of charts to present information diagrammatically is discussed and simple methods of summarizing data are examined. These are the minimum tools that the small-scale quantitative researcher needs. There are many other statistical methods that might be useful, but a description of these is beyond the scope of this chapter. The use of computers and computer packages is unlikely to be cost effective in small-scale investigations, and so the computer analysis of results is not discussed.

The Nature of Data

In designing a questionnaire or interview schedule, the investigator must plan for the analysis stage in case the point is reached where the data collected are unsuitable for the method of analysis required. It is important to know that there are different types of data. There are different scales of measurement:

Nominal scales are the simplest and arise where simple categories with no numerical significance are used. For example, an item on a questionnaire may require a 'yes' or 'no' response. For the purpose of coding, we may attach numbers to these:

response	yes	no
code	1	2

This is known as the coding frame for the question.

The important point about nominal scales is that these numbers (the codes) are completely arbitrary and are merely labelling devices. Classification-type questions such as 'main subject taught' will also lead to a coding frame consisting of categories to which numbers may be ascribed: these numbers will constitute a nominal scale of measurement.

Ordinal scales arise where items are rated or ranked. A coding frame for questions of opinion might be:

strongly disagree	disagree	neutral	agree	strongly agree
1	2	3	4	5

The implication here is that the higher the category chosen the greater the strength of agreement. A classification question regarding the grade of teacher or lecturer would also involve an ordinal scale: a scale 3 post has a higher status than a scale 1 or 2, but not such a high status as a scale 4. Ordinal scales distinguish order but nothing can be said about how much larger one item is than another, simply that it is larger.

Interval scales are more sophisticated than ordinal scales. Examination marks, IQ and other measures of performance are usually regarded as following an interval scale of measurement. If pupil A achieves a mark of 60 per cent, pupil B 45 per cent and pupil C 30 per cent in a particular examination, then the implication of an interval scale is first, that A is more proficient than B, who is more proficient than C in the subject being examined; second, A's greater proficiency than B's (60 per cent against 45 per cent) is equal to B's greater proficiency than C's (45 per cent against 30 per cent).

Note, however, that it cannot be said that A is twice as proficient as C even though numerically 60 is twice 30. This is because the range of the examination marks, 0–100, does not represent the full range of ability. A pupil who receives full marks is not deemed to know all there is to know about the particular subject; further, he or she may know far more than the examination tests. At best it can be assumed that A knows as much more than B as B does than C. Equal intervals, therefore, represent equal amounts.

Ratio scales are the highest order of measurement. Measurements such as age, salary and so on follow ratio scales. As with interval scales, equal differences represent equal amounts. However, in ratio scales, absolute measurements are valid. For example, a person who is fifty years old has lived twice as long as someone who is twenty-five years old. This property applies only to ratio scales.

As well as there being different scales of measurement, variables (characteristics which are measured on any of the above scales) may also be classified as discrete or continuous. A variable is said to be *discrete* if it can only take whole number values; for example, the size of each section of the library — only whole numbers of books are counted. A variable which can take any value is *continuous*; for example, the age of a person — a member of staff may be twenty-eight years of age or thirty-five and a half years.

Distinctions are sometimes drawn between qualitative variables and quantitative variables; the former usually refer to characteristics measured on nominal or ordinal scales (e.g. responses to questions of opinion), whereas the latter refer to data measured on interval or ratio scales (e.g. age, income).

What's All the Fuss About?

As we start to look at how data may be summarized, it should become clearer as to the importance of understanding the different types of data. There are methods which can only be applied to data conforming to ratio and interval scales: it is not normally regarded as appropriate, for instance, to use averages with ordinal scales.

Four questions (Figure 11.1) based on those used by Bradley and Silverleaf (1979) in their study of careers in further education teaching are used to illustrate the various methods available. Bradley and Silverleaf's was a large-scale investigation but the questions selected are ones that could be employed in a study of staff development in a school or college. The data used are fictitious and for the purpose of the illustrations are taken to be derived from staff of a single department in a college of further education.

For each question, please circle the number which corresponds with your answer:

Are there sufficient opportunities in your present position to improve your qualifications?

Yes	No
1	2

I consider my promotion prospects within the college to be good:

strongly disagree	disagree	neutral	agree	strongly agree
1	2	3	4	5

Since the age of eighteen, how many years did you spend in employment in the following fields before entering further education teaching?
(please exclude vacation, casual and part-time work)

	None	1–5	6–10	over 10	(No. of years)
School teaching	1	2	3	4	
Industry, commerce	1	2	3	4	
Civil Service, local government	1	2	3	4	
Research	1	2	3	4	
Other	1	2	3	4	

Age last birthday

25–29	30–34	35–39	40–44	45–49	50–54	55–59
1	2	3	4	5	6	7

Figure 11.1 Extract of questionnaire.

Recording the Information

The importance of planning the analysis of the questionnaire responses in advance cannot be overemphasized. The preparation of summary sheets, onto which all questionnaire responses can be transferred, does in itself highlight ways in which the questionnaire might be simplified.

The summary sheets should, therefore, be prepared at the same time as the questionnaire. One way of drafting the summary sheets would be as shown in Figure 11.2.

Respondent	Question 1 1 2	Question 2 1 2 3 4 5	Question 3 1 2 3 4	

Figure 11.2   Example of a summary sheet.

The first column of the summary sheet is for the respondent's name, or better still his or her 'number' (see below). The responses to each section are coded such that, for example, question 1 requires a response of 'yes' (coded 1) or 'no' (coded 2); question 2 may be an opinion question requiring the respondent to indicate strong disagreement (coded 1), disagreement (coded 2) or strong agreement (coded 5).

When the completed questionnaires are returned they can be numbered for identification purposes. If the subsequent analysis is to involve comparisons between different groups of staff (e.g. with respect to grade or sex or age), then the numbering should, as far as simplicity permits, identify each respondent as such. For example, 01/HOD/F might be the 'number' for the completed questionnaire from the respondent 01, who is the female head of department. 02/PL/M would then be the label for the questionnaire from respondent 02, who is a male principal lecturer.

The questionnaires must be checked for completeness: it may be possible to return to the respondent if there have been omissions. The responses to the questions can then be coded (i.e. the appropriate code allocated to the responses), or if the questions have all been pre-coded, responses can be transferred to the summary sheet.

Open-ended questions need careful handling; it is possible that the responses to these can be classified after all the questionnaires have been returned, in which case a coding frame can be drawn up and the responses coded. It is more likely perhaps that investigators will wish to report word-for-word responses to open-ended questions of opinion; in this case, responses should be written out on separate sheets for each question and included selectively in the report. The basis for inclusion in the report should be the same as for any data collected — to provide a representative view of the responses obtained.

Once the completed questionnaires have been coded, then the responses can be transferred from the questionnaires to the summary sheets using ticks (Fig 11.3).

Respondent	Question 1		Question 2	Question 3	
	1	2	1 2 3 4 5	1 2 3 4	
01/HOD/F	✓		✓		
02/PL/M	✓		✓		
03/SL/M		✓	✓		

Figure 11.3   Completing the summary sheet.

The process of transferring responses to summary sheets is tedious, but the alternatives are either more tedious or prone to error or both. Once the information from the questionnaires is recorded on the summary sheets in a systematic way such as has been described then it should be unnecessary to consult the questionnaires again, but they should not be discarded until the report is finalized, just in case checking is needed.

After Recording

The following examples illustrate the different ways in which the information collected may be analysed and presented. For this question, the analysis of the nominal data collected is a simple matter of totalling on the summary sheet the 'yes' responses (coded 1) and the 'no' responses (coded 2). If out of the forty staff in the department who responded, ten had responded 'yes' and thirty had responded 'no', then these frequencies, as they are called, can be converted to percentages of the total number.

Are there sufficient opportunities in your present position to improve your qualifications?

> Yes   1
> No   2

For the 'yes' responses $\dfrac{10}{40} \times 100 = 25\%$

For the 'no' responses $\dfrac{30}{40} \times 100 = 75\%$

So 25 per cent of the department's staff feel that there are sufficient opportunities to improve their qualifications, whilst 75 per cent think that there are not.

If it is relevant to the study, it is possible to examine the variation in the response to this question according to the grade of the respondent or the gender. With small groups it is important not to carry these comparisons too far. If senior departmental staff are regarded as senior lecturers and above, and their responses to the given question are separated from those of lecturers grade II and from those of lecturers grade I, then the cross-tabulation shown in Table 11.1. might result.

Table 11.1   Teachers' perceptions of the sufficiency of opportunities to improve their own qualifications

	Sufficient	*Insufficient*	*Total*
Senior staff*	4	1	5
Lecturers grade II	3	12	15
Lecturers grade I	3	17	20
	10	30	40

* Senior lecturers and above

The table shows actual frequencies rather than percentages. Where there are small total numbers, beware of using percentages. A statement such as '80 per cent of the senior staff feel that there are sufficient opportunities to improve their qualifications' is factually accurate, but it is *misleading* as the reader will assume a much larger total number of senior staff than five. It would be better to include the tabulation in the report and to draw out differences of opinions using the actual frequencies. The following statement would be appropriate: 'Whereas four out of the five senior staff in the department feel that there are sufficient opportunities to improve their qualifications, only three out of 15 lecturers grade II and three out of 20 lecturers grade I feel that the opportunities are sufficient.' The variable here, attitude towards promotion prospects, is being measured on an ordinal scale. It is a simple task to determine the frequencies of each value: the numbers or respondents giving each answer are totalled on the summary sheet. The results might be as shown in Table 11.2.

Example 2

I consider my promotion prospects within the college to be good:				
strongly disagree	disagree	neutral	agree	strongly agree
1	2	3	4	5

Table 11.2 Levels of agreement amongst staff that promotion prospects within the college are good

Strongly disagree	Disagree	Neutral	Agree	Stongly agree	Total
10	20	6	2	2	40

These frequencies may be converted to percentages to illustrate the relative levels of agreement, and the following statement might be used, accompanied by the table, in the report: 'Only 10 per cent (four out of forty) of the department's staff felt any measure of agreement with the statement that 'I consider promotion prospects within the college to be good' whereas 50 per cent (twenty out of forty) disagreed and a further 25 per cent (ten out of forty) strongly disagreed.'

A bar chart could be used as an alternative method of presentation in the report (Figure 11.4). The researcher has to make a judgement as to which presentation is the clearest.

For vertical bar charts such as the one shown in Figure 11.4, the variable is placed on the horizontal axis and the frequency on the upright axis; horizontal bar charts are presented the other way round (see Figure 11.6). For precision the actual frequencies are included at the tops of the bars and the total frequency of forty is stated in the conventional form 'n = 40' (n stands for number). The important point to note, and this is a principle which should guide the construction of all bar charts, is that the area of the bars on the chart should be proportional to the frequencies they represent, so the height of the bar representing the number who strongly disagree (ten) is half the height of the bar representing the number who disagree (twenty), the width of the bars being the same. It follows from this that the frequency axis of bar charts should always start from zero, in order that the presentation does not give the wrong impression.

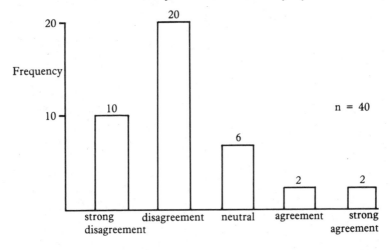

Figure 11.4 Levels of agreement amongst staff that promotion prospects within the college are good.

As in the previous example, the investigator may wish to compare the responses to this question according to the grade of the member of staff. The resulting cross-tabulation might be as in Table 11.3.

Table 11.3 Levels of agreement amongst staff, by grade, that promotion prospects within the college are good

	Strongly disagree	Disagree	Neutral	Agree	Stongly agree	Total
Senior staff*	0	2	2	0	1	5
Lecturers grade II	4	6	3	1	1	15
Lecturers grade I	6	12	1	1	0	20
	10	20	6	2	2	40

* Senior lecturer or over.

Figure 11.5 is an alternative representation to the tabulation; it is generally regarded as unnecessary to include both a tabulation and chart of the same data. Figure 11.5 is an example of a compound bar chart: it compares the frequencies, by grade, of attitudes towards promotion prospects. For each category of agreement/disagreement, the frequencies of the different staff groups are shown side by side. The

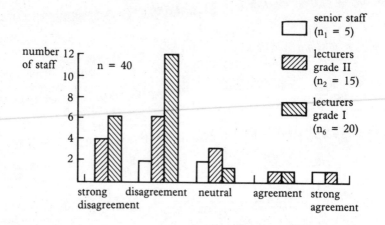

Figure 11.5 Levels of agreement amongst staff, by grade, that promotion prospects within the college are good

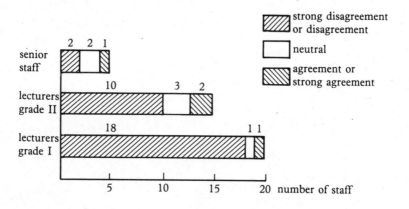

Figure 11.6 Staff attitudes towards the statement that promotion prospects within the college are good.

order of these groups is maintained throughout the diagram: in this case, senior staff, lecturers grade II, lecturers grade I. A further alternative method of presentation is a component bar chart (Fig. 11.6). This is presented as a horizontal bar chart. Notice that the total lengths of the bars represent the number of staff in each grade. For the sake of simplicity the categories have been collapsed into three: disagreement (strong or otherwise); neutral; agreement (strong or otherwise).

The method of presentation chosen (tabulation, compound bar chart or component bar chart) depends on the point that is being made in the report: the table or chart should illustrate that point. If the object is to show the overall view about promotion prospects, then Figure 11.4 would be appropriate. If, however, the object is to show how the different groups of staff vary in their views about promotion prospects then Figures 11.5 or 11.6 would be preferred.

In example 3 respondents are being asked to circle the code against the different employment sectors to indicate the number of years' experience they have had in each. In effect, there are five questions here: respondents are being asked to state the number of years' experience they have had school teaching, the number of years' experience they have had in industry/commerce, and so on. The responses would be transferred to the summary sheet as if the question were delivered five times — once for each employment sector. As before, the responses can be totalled and presented in the report in the form of a table (Table 11.4). In this case those respondents not having work experience in a particular employment sector are excluded. Note that if a member of staff has had experience as a school teacher, then he or she may also have worked in industry or local government; note also that some staff may not have had any work experience prior to entering further education teaching. The totals, therefore, have a different meaning from in the earlier examples. In all, thirteen staff have worked as school teachers prior to entering the further education teaching profession, whereas thirty-three out of the forty staff have worked in industry or commerce and thirteen have experience of civil service or local government.

Example 3

	None	1–5	6–10	Over 10 (No. of years)
Since the age of 18, how many years did you spend in employment in the following fields before entering further education teaching? (please exclude vacation, casual and part-time work)				
School teaching	1	2	3	4
Industry, commerce	1	2	3	4
Civil service, local government	1	2	3	4
Research	1	2	3	4
Other	1	2	3	4

If a chart is preferred to a tabulation in the project report, then a compound bar chart such as in Figure 11.7 might be used.

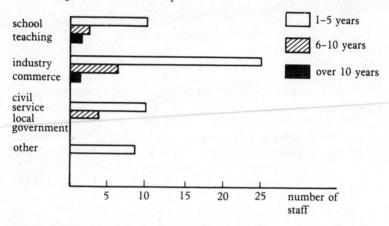

Figure 11.7 Work experience of staff.

If the investigator wishes to illustrate the relative numbers of staff having experience in the employment sectors and wishes to show the length of service too, then a percentage component bar chart (Fig. 11.8) might be used. The frequencies have been converted to percentages of the total staff (forty). This representation, by implication, also shows the percentage of staff not having experience in each sector. Note, however, that none of these representations reveals the number of staff who have had no work experience prior to entering further education teaching.

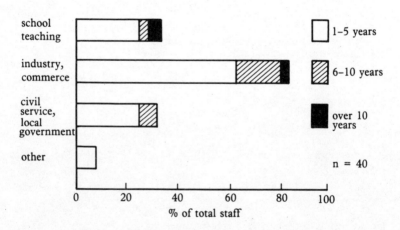

Figure 11.8 Percentage of staff having work experience, by sector.

It might be of interest to compare the work experience of the different categories of staff, that is according to their grade or gender. This might be considered overelaborate in the context of a small-scale survey but it really does depend on what the investigator is seeking to show in the report.

A method of presentation in wide usage is the pie chart (Fig. 11.9). Separate pies might be drawn to show the work experience in the different sectors. Pie charts are easily understood but not so easily constructed. As with bar charts, the areas of the pie are proportional to the amounts they represent. The whole pie in Figure 11.9 represents 100 per cent, that is all of the staff in the department. The unshaded segment represents the percentage with no industrial/commercial work experience: the size of it is determined by finding 17.5 per cent of 360 (the number of degrees in a circle). This number of degrees (63°) is measured using a protractor starting from the twelve o'clock position. The other segments are constructed in a similar manner. Pies representing the work experience in the other employment sectors would be drawn with the same diameters since the total number (n = 40) is the same throughout. Where pies are to represent different totals, then the sizes of the pies should be adjusted accordingly.

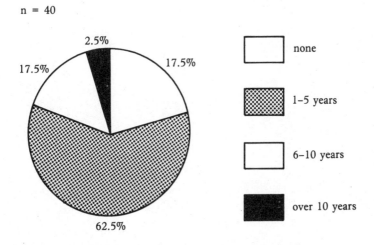

Figure 11.9   Percentage of staff having work experience in industry/commerce.

In example 4, classification-type questions of a personal nature, such as age, produce a higher response rate where categories are used rather than the respondents' being asked, 'How old are you?' In any case, data have to be grouped to enable a pattern to be seen. The classes chosen (25–29, 30–34, 35–39, etc.) must, as in any coding frame, cover the full range of ages of the department's staff, and they must be unambiguous so it is clear to respondents into which categories their ages fall. Note that the categories are such that they each span five years: 25–29 includes the ages of all staff who are just twenty-five years old up to those who are very nearly thirty years; this span is known as the class interval. In this example all the class intervals are five years; if it is possible, then equal intervals throughout are desirable.

Example 4

Age last birthday						
25–29	30–34	35–39	40–44	45–49	50–54	55–59
1	2	3	4	5	6	7

The frequencies of each class are determined from the summary sheet and form what is known as a frequency distribution (Table 11.5).

Table 11.5   Age distribution of staff

Years	Frequency
25–29	2
30–34	9
35–39	10
40–44	7
45–49	5
50–54	4
55–59	3
	40

It may be represented by means of a frequency histogram (Fig. 11.10): this term is used for a simple vertical bar chart, depicting the class frequencies of a quantitative variable.

Note that the variable (age) is continuous; it does not just take whole number values: it is merely a matter of convenience that age is often recorded to the nearest year. Hence, the labelling of the horizontal axis: the variable is continuous so there are no gaps between the bars. For the sake of simplicity, the precise limits between classes are merged on the histogram.

The frequency distribution and its representation by means of a histogram provide a picture of the age structure of the department, and either or both might be included in the project report. The diagram helps to identify important aspects of the data. A comment on the features of the age structure represented in Figure 11.10 might be as follows: 'The ages of the department's staff vary from under thirty to over fifty-five with 65 per cent of the staff being aged between thirty and forty-five.'

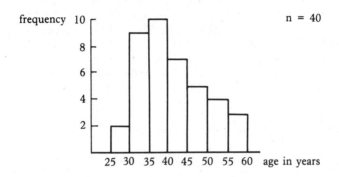

Figure 11.10   Age distribution of staff.

What about Averages?

Since the variable, age, is measured on a ratio scale, more sophisticated statistical methods are available. An average age of the department's staff may be determined. There are different types of average (more properly known as measures of location or central tendency) and circumstances determine which is the most appropriate. Three measures of location are considered here: the mode, the median and the mean; the criteria for deciding which should be used when, are discussed later.

The mode is the most frequently occurring value, or in the case of grouped data, the modal class is the one which has the highest frequency. By reference to Table 11.5, it can be seen that the modal age group is 35–39, that is the age group 35–39 contains the largest number of staff. The mode is a very simple measure which can be used even where a variable is measured on a nominal scale; for example, eye colouring — if more people have green eyes than any other colour, then the modal eye colour is green.

The median is a different type of average: it is the value below which half the data lie and above which the other half lie. Put another way, the median is the middle value when the data are listed in order.

The easiest way to calculate the median from a set of grouped data is, first, to calculate the cumulative class frequencies and, second, to plot these by means of a cumulative frequency polygon (otherwise known as an ogive), from which the median can be determined. What follows illustrates this procedure.

Table 11.6 shows the results of accumulating the frequencies taken from Table 11.5. The number of staff who are less than thirty years of age (the upper limit of the 20–29 class) is two; the number of staff who are less than thirty-five years (the upper limit of the next class) is equal to the sum of the frequencies of the first two classes (2 + 9); the number of staff who are less than forty years is equal to the frequencies of the first three classes and so on. The cumulative frequency of the upper limit of the last class is forty, that is all the staff are under sixty years of age.

Table 11.6 Cumulative frequency distribution of ages of staff

Upper class limit	Cumulative frequency
30	2
35	11
40	21
45	28
50	33
55	37
60	40

The cumulative frequency polygon (Fig. 11.11) is constructed from the cumulative frequency distribution (Table 11.6). The vertical axis represents cumulative frequency and the horizontal axis, the variable (in this case, age). The cumulative frequencies are then plotted against the upper class limits.

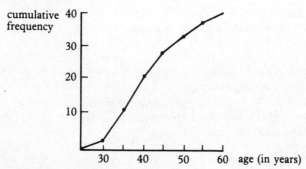

Figure 11.11 Cumulative frequency polygon of the age distribution of staff

Note that a zero cumulative frequency is plotted against the lower limit of the first class. It is now a simple matter to determine the median. The median is the middle value, so since there are forty staff, the median age is the age of the twentieth member of staff when the ages are listed in order. The cumulative frequency distribution and polygon have put the data in order, so to find the age of the twentieth member of staff, a line is drawn horizontally from the cumulative frequency of 20 as far as the polygon (Fig. 11.12); a vertical line is dropped from this point on the polygon to the horizontal axis. The position at which this vertical line intersects the horizontal axis is the value of the median. From Figure 11.12 it can be seen that the median is thirty-nine years, that is the average age, as measured by the median, is thirty-nine years; half the staff are younger than thirty-nine, half are older.

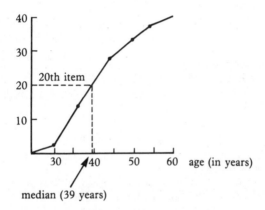

Figure 11.12 Cumulative frequency polygon of the age distribution of staff, showing the median.

By definition, a median can only exist for data which can be placed in order; hence the median can only be used for variables which follow ordinal, interval and ratio scales.

The arithmetic mean, or simply the mean, is a third measure of location. Where data are ungrouped then the mean is the sum of these individual items divided by the number of items. For example, if the IQs of five children are 108, 95, 118, 99, 110, and if

$$\text{the arithmetic mean} = \frac{\text{sum of values}}{\text{number of subjects}} \text{, and}$$

the sum of the IQs is 530 (108+95+118+99+110) and the number of subjects is five, then the arithmetic mean $= \dfrac{530}{5} = 106$

that is, the mean IQ of these five children is 106.

Statistical notation allows us to write down a formula for the arithmetic mean. If x represents the variable, which takes the values x_1, x_2, x_3, x_4 . . . and n is the number of items, the arithmetic mean is denoted by $\bar{x}$ (x-bar) and the formula is:

$\bar{x} = \dfrac{\Sigma x}{n}$ where Σx is the notation* for the sum of the values of x.

that is, the mean (x) $= \dfrac{\text{sum of the values}}{\text{no. of items}} = \dfrac{\Sigma x}{n}$.

When the data are grouped as in Table 11.5, there is a need to take into account the frequency of the classes (f). Table 11.7 shows the steps involved in calculating the mean from grouped data. The first class 25–29 has a frequency, f, of 2; for the purpose of calculating the mean, it is assumed that both of these items of data are at the mid-point of the class (i.e. 27.5 — remember the upper limit of the class is 30). The second class has a frequency of 9 and the mid-point is 32.5 and so on. The mean for these grouped data is calculated, first by multiplying the frequency, f, of each class by its mid-point, x; second, these products are totalled, and third this total is divided by the total frequency. So for grouped data

$$\bar{x} = \frac{\Sigma fx}{\Sigma f}$$

i.e. the mean $(\bar{x}) =$

$\dfrac{\text{the sum of the products of the class frequencies (f) and the mid-points (x)}}{\text{the total frequency } (\Sigma f)}$

Table 11.7   Calculation of the mean from a set of grouped data

Classes	Mid-points x	Frequency f	Frequency × mid-point f × x
25–29	27.5	2	55
30–34	32.5	9	292.5
35–39	37.5	10	375
40–44	42.5	7	297.5
45–49	47.5	5	237.5
50–54	52.5	4	210
54–59	57.5	3	172.5
		$\Sigma f = 40$	$\Sigma fx = 1640$

* Σ is the Greek capital letter sigma, s, standing for summation.

Mean, $\bar{x} = \dfrac{\Sigma fx}{\Sigma f} = \dfrac{1640}{40} = 41$

The mean age of the department's staff is forty-one years.

Which Average?

For the purpose of illustration, the mode, median and mean have all been calculated from the age distribution in Table 11.5. In practice only one of these would be used. The question of which average to use depends on the shape of the distribution. The shape of the frequency distribution in Figure 11.10 is somewhat lop-sided or skewed; other distributions are more symmetrical. A general guideline is that data on ratio or interval scales which are distributed in a symmetrical or near symmetrical way should be summarized using the arithmetic mean. The reason for this is that the mean is a very powerful measure which takes into account all items of data but which is distorted if there are odd extreme values; a symmetrical distribution does not, however, distort the mean.

Data on ratio, interval or ordinal scales which follow an asymmetrical (or skewed) distribution should be summarized using the median; the median is not affected by extreme values and for non-symmetrical distributions provides an average that is more typical of the data. The mode may be useful for nominal and discrete data.

Measures of Dispersion

Measures of dispersion quantify the variability within a set of data. It was seen earlier that the mean age of staff in the fictitious department was forty-one years; without reference to the frequency distribution (Table 11.5), it is not possible to tell whether staff are mostly aged between, say, thirty-five and forty-five or whether their ages vary more widely. Measures of dispersion, therefore, are used in addition to measures of location (types of average) to summarize a set of data. Just as comparisons may be made between two groups by examining, say, the average age of each, then so may they be compared in terms of the variability of the ages in each using measures of dispersion.

There are many statistical books which explain how measures of dispersion such as the range, the interquartile range and the standard deviation may be determined, and it is not intended to explain here their calculation. Suffice to say that if the median is used as the most appropriate measure of location to summarize a set of data, then the interquartile range may be used as well to measure the variation in the data. Similarly, where the mean is used, then the standard deviation is the appropriate measure of dispersion. The range is a very simple measure of dispersion — it is the difference between the lowest and the highest item of data. It is a rather crude measure but may be useful where data are evenly spread and there are no extreme values.

Conclusion

Descriptive statistical methods are wide-ranging. This chapter has attempted to show some of the simple ways in which information can be collated, analysed and presented. There are many more sophisticated techniques. The methods suggested are not meant to be exhaustive — the researcher may well be able to present results in a novel manner. Where a single measure (or measures) or a diagram can be used to present in a simple and straightforward way a concept, a pattern or a set of data, then it is usually preferable to pages of written description.

Analysis and Presentation of Information Checklist

1. Results of small-scale studies will generally be illuminative rather than generalizable.

   Descriptive statistical methods are likely to be most useful. They provide 'pictures' of the group under investigation.

2. Plan for analysis at the design stage.

3. There are different scales of measurement.

   Nominal scales are simplest. They arise where simple categories with no numerical significance are used. *Ordinal scales* arise where items are ranked or rated.
   Interval scales are more sophisticated. Examination marks, IQ and other measures of performance are usually regarded as following an interval scale of measurement.
   Ratio scales are the highest order of measurement. Age, salary etc. follow ratio scales.

4. *Variables* (characteristics which are measured on any of the above scales of measurement) may be classified as *discrete* or *continuous*.

   A variable is discrete if it can only take whole numbers; it is continuous if it can take any value.

5. Prepare summary sheets for questionnaire analysis.

   Number questionnaires. Identify respondents.

6. Decide what to do about open-ended responses.

Classify and draw up a coding frame? Report responses verbatim? If the latter, write out responses on separate sheets.

7. Code questionnaires.

Transfer responses from the questionnaires to the summary sheets.

8. Produce frequencies and/or percentages, if appropriate.

Beware of using percentages where there are small total numbers.

9. Consider the best way to present the information.

Percentages? Bar charts? Cross tabulation? Compound bar charts? Component bar charts? Tables? Pie charts? Histograms? Cumulative frequency polygons?

10. If averages (more properly known as measures of location or central tendency) are calculated, decide which type is the most appropriate.

Mode, median or mean? Circumstances determine which is the most appropriate.

11. Select and present results in a way which will be clear to readers and which will draw attention to key factors.

Where a single measure (or measures) or a diagram can be used to present in a simple and straightforward way a concept, a pattern or a set of data, then it is usually preferable to pages of written description.

12

Writing the Report

Getting Started

When all the hard work of gathering and analysing evidence is complete, you will need to write the final report. Bogdan and Biklen, writing about the problems of getting started, offer the following advice:

> Novice writers are big procrastinators. They find countless reasons not to get started. Even when they finally get themselves seated at their desks, they always seem to find diversions: make the coffee, sharpen the pencil, go to the bathroom, thumb through more literature, sometimes even get up and return to the field. Remember that you are never 'ready' to write; writing is something you must make a conscious decision to do and then discipline yourself to follow through.
>
> (Bogdan and Biklen 1982:172)

All this is easier said than done, and it is not only novice writers who are procrastinators, but remember that a study is not finished until it is written up and, in your original planning, time has to be allowed for writing. That does not mean that you put off thoughts of writing until all the data have been collected. If you have followed some of the earlier advice, you will already have produced an evaluation of what you have read about the topic, so you will not have to waste time going back to books and articles read some time ago. You will have your bibliographical cards in good order, with notes and useful quotations to guide your writing, and you will not have started your project unless your objectives were clear, though you may have amended your objectives as your investigation developed.

Report writing is not, or should not be, a frantic activity carried out at the end of the project. It is a process of varied stages all of which need to be recorded at the time they are completed. Your first drafts will almost certainly need to be revised and in some cases completely rewritten, but the foundations for the report should have been established at the planning stage.

Writing a report or a dissertation requires discipline and even the most experienced of researchers need to impose some sort of self-control to ensure that the task is completed on time. We all have different ways of working and what suits one person may not suit another. By a method of trial and error, you will need to work out what is best for you, but the following guidelines, which derive largely from Barzun and Graff (1977), may provide a starting point for working out your own writing plan:

1. *Set deadlines:* You will already have set deadlines and completion dates for different sections and for the whole report in your original schedule, but plans and ideas do sometimes change during the course of an investigation. With the help of your supervisor, set a deadline for the completion of the writing and keep that date constantly in mind.

2. *Write regularly:* Many researchers find that they need to keep regular hours and to work in the same place. They find that building up an association between work and a particular place eases the difficulty of starting to write. The aim is never to miss a writing session.

3. *Create a rhythm of work:* Barzun and Graff (1977:325) suggest that the periods of writing should be 'close enough to create a rhythm of work'. It is tempting to stop to check a reference or because you have written a certain number of words that would seem to justify breaking off at that point, but resist the temptation. Keep the momentum going.

4. *Write up a section as soon as it is ready:* Some sections of the research will be ready for writing up before others. Whatever sequence is attempted, it is a good idea to aim at writing a minimum number of words in each writing session.

5. *Stop at a point from which it is easy to resume writing:* If you stop at a point when the next passage is difficult, it may discourage you from resuming work promptly for the next session. It is better to stop at a point when the next session's writing can get off to a running start.

6. *Leave space for revisions:* You will almost certainly need to revise and rewrite, so write only one paragraph on each page so that you can move paragraphs around if necessary. Remember also to write on only one side of each page.

7. *Publicize your plans:* You may need some help from family and friends to complete your report on time. We can all find good reasons for not getting down to writing, so tell everyone about your writing routine. With any luck, they will not tempt you with invitations to the pub or incite you to watch television. They may in fact put pressure on you to get to your desk. As Barzun and Graff (1977:325) emphasize, 'The writer's problem is the inverse of the reformed drunkard's. The latter must never touch a drop; the former must always do his stint.'

Structuring the Report

Opinions vary as to the order in which sections should appear, but most researchers would agree with Nisbet and Entwistle (1970:168) that a report or dissertation should include the following major sections:

1. Outline of the research.
2. Review of previous work.
3. Precise statement of the scope and aims of the investigation.
4. Description of the procedure, sample and tests of measurements used (if any).
5. Statement of results.
6. Discussion.
7. Summary and conclusions.
8   References.

Many institutions also ask for an abstract, and so the final task should be to produce a brief, succinct statement which indicates what the research set out to do, the methods used and the results obtained.

1. *Outline of the Research*

The main aim of this short section is to give a clear picture of the aims, methods and results of the research. It is intended to provide a frame of reference which will allow the nature of the research to be taken in quickly. Arguments and discussions are out of place here and only the essential points of the research should be indicated.

You may find it best to write this section last, to ensure that it accurately reflects what is in the main body of the report.

2. *Review of Previous Research*

Not all reports will include a review of previous research, though most will. You may have used your background reading mainly to support arguments throughout the report, but the value of a review to the reader is that it explains the context and background of the study. Remember Haywood and Wragg's warning that critical reviews can too often turn out to be uncritical reviews — 'the furniture sale catalogue, in which everything merits a one-paragraph entry no matter how skilfully it has been conducted' (Haywood and Wragg 1982:2). Selection has to be made, and only books and articles which relate directly to the topic should be included. Do you recall Woodley's (1985) review of the literature relating to mature students, discussed in Chapter 3 (see pp 20/21). He selected from an extensive amount of literature only material which related to his own study. He grouped certain categories, commented on features which were of particular importance, compared the results of different investigators and discussed in some detail a study by Walker (1975), which served as a pilot study for his own research. In his review of the literature, he set the scene, placed his own work in context and prepared the reader for what was to follow.

The literature review can be written first and, if you have managed to discipline yourself sufficiently well to write up sections and sub-sections as you have completed them, much of the work of this section will be ready for revision before you begin to collect data. You may find that you need to adapt your original version, but you should not need to start from the beginning by reading through notes to decide what should be included and what left out.

3. *Precise Statement of the Scope and Aims of the Investigation*

This should be a brief explanation of the purpose of the research. Explain the research problem in a few sentences and mention the proposed contribution to practical or theoretical issues. Draw attention to any limitations of the study at this stage. An individual researcher with only 100 hours or so to complete a project cannot hope to become involved in complex sampling techniques nor to interview hundreds of people. You cannot do everything in a small study, and your supervisor will know that, but in this section you should make it clear that you know what the limitations of your study are.

As in section 1, you will have considered and possibly outlined this section earlier in the project, but it is probably best to write the first version of section 3 last, together with section 1.

4. *Description of the Procedure, Sample and Tests of Measurement Used (if Any)*

This section explains how the problem was investigated and why particular methods and techniques were employed. Accounts of the procedure, size of sample, method of selection, choice of variables and controls, and tests of measurement and statistical analyses, if any, should be provided.

Nisbet and Entwistle (1970:169) point out that it is unnecessary to describe in detail any standard tests or procedures that are well known and about which further information can easily be obtained, but if subjective assessments or individually devised measurement techniques have been used, then some explanation is necessary.

All important terms and variables should be defined precisely (Turney and Robb 1971:175) and any deficiencies in the methods mentioned. It is important to bear in mind that in certain kinds of investigation, the research needs to be repeatable, and a fellow researcher should be able to obtain enough information from this section to make this possible.

5.   *Statement of Results*

This is the heart of the report and will consist of tables or figures and text, depending on the nature of the project. Before you start this chapter, refresh your memory by reading Chapter 11, 'Analysis and Presentation of Information'. The way results are presented is important. Tables, charts, graphs and other figures should illustrate and illuminate the text. If they do not, then there is no point in taking up space. The text, which should be written after the results are prepared, should not duplicate information in the tables and figures but should highlight significant aspects of the findings (Travers 1964:526) so that all relevant facts are presented in a way which draws the reader's attention to what is most important. It is quite an art to achieve this balance, and you may find you need several drafts before you are satisfied with the result.

6.   *Analysis and Discussion*

It is often best to start this section with a restatement of the problem before discussing how the results affect existing knowledge of the subject. If your research aimed to test certain hypotheses, then this section should demonstrate whether they were or were not supported by the evidence. Any deficiencies in the research design should be mentioned, with suggestions about different approaches which might have been more appropriate. Implications for improvement of educational practice, if any, should also be drawn out.

Most researchers find it best to write sections 4, 5 and 6 in sequence to ensure continuity and logical progression. It is quite feasible to write some sections as discrete units at different times, but these three sections need to be considered as a whole. If you have to take a break from writing, make sure you reread everything that had gone before to ensure a smooth continuation and to avoid repetition.

7.   *Summary and Conclusions*

The main conclusions of the report that have been discussed in section 6 should be summarized here briefly and simply. Only conclusions that can be justifiably drawn from the findings should be made. That sounds (and is) obvious, but there is often a great temptation to drop in an opinion for which no evidence is provided in the report. Take care or you may spoil a good report by including a throwaway remark.

Before you write this section, read through the whole report and make a note of key points. Readers who want a quick idea of what your research is about will look at the abstract, possibly the introduction and almost certainly at the summary and conclusions. This final section should be sufficiently succinct and clearly expressed to enable readers to understand quite clearly what research has been done and the conclusions that have been drawn from the evidence.

8. List of References

All reports will require a bibliography, a list of references, or both. The term 'bibliography' has several meanings. It can be used to mean a publication listing the details of material about a subject, place or person. It can be a list of works by a specific author or it can be a list of sources consulted during the preparation of an essay, project or dissertation. It you are asked to produce a bibliography for your report, that will obviously mean that you are to provide a list of sources.

Lists of references are different. They will give specific details only about books and articles which have been cited or referred to in the report. Apart from page references to journals, page numbers are not included in bibliographies, but they may be included, where appropriate, in references. If you adopt the Harvard method, then references will appear in alphabetical order, which simplifies the process and avoids overlap. If you adopt the British or another numerical system, then references will appear in the order in which they appeared in the text.

The amount of time it takes you to produce either or both in your final report will depend on how meticulous you were when you made out your reference cards. This is the time when hard work and systematic recording really pay off.

The Mechanics of Presenting a Report

Length

Guidelines about length will be provided by your supervisor, and many institutions produce leaflets which give information about the nuts and bolts of presenting a report. If you have not been told what length is expected, ask. If a maximum number of words is stipulated, stick to that number. You may be penalized for exceeding the limit.

Title Page

Include a title page, incorporating the title of your study and your name. The title should accurately reflect the nature of your study and should be brief and to the point. A main title and subtitle may be provided if the subtitle clarifies the purpose of the study.

Acknowledgements and Thanks

You may wish to acknowledge the help given to you in the preparation of your report. If so, acknowledgements and thanks come after the title page.

Headings

Include section headings where possible. They help the reader to follow your structure and arguments.

Tables and Figures

Not all reports will have tables and figures, but if these are to be included, they should be numbered, given a title and carefully checked before you send off your report for marking. (Tables are generally numerical presentations, in lists or columns, though there can be tables of names or other items. Figures are other types of presentation of data).

Quotations

All quotations must be acknowledged. Remember that your tutor has probably read the same books, so is likely to recognize the source. If you are quoting only a few words or one sentence, it will be sufficient to indicate this by using inverted commas in the main text, with the source in brackets. If words are missed out of the quotation, indicate by three full stops. For example, as Hopkins (1985:78) says, 'Documents . . . can illuminate rationale and purpose in interesting ways.' If the quotation is longer, indent it and (if the report is typed), use single spacing.

As Hopkins says:

> Documents (memos, letters, position papers, examination papers, newspaper clippings, etc.) surrounding a curriculum or other educational concern can illuminate rationale and purpose in interesting ways. The use of such material can provide background information and understanding of issues that would not otherwise be available.

(Hopkins, 1985: 78)

Some institutional guidelines ask you to put quotation marks at the beginning and end of each longer quotation; others do not, so follow the 'house' rules.

Appendices

Copies of research instruments (questionnaires, interview schedules etc.) that have been used should be included in an appendix, unless you have been instructed otherwise. Your tutor will not wish to receive all completed questionnaires and would no doubt be dismayed if weighty parcels arrived on the doorstep, but one copy of any data collecting instrument that has been used is generally required.

The Abstract

In most cases, an abstract will be required, though again, practices vary so consult the 'house' rules. It is quite difficult to say in a few words what your investigation set out to do, the methods employed and what conclusions were reached. You may need several attempts before you achieve a sufficiently brief yet informative statement. The following example fulfils all the requirements of an abstract, and might serve as a model.

This case study is an investigation into how the governing body of one comprehensive school defines its role in relation to the curriculum. It attempts to identify the influences and constraints which affect the way in which the role of the governing body is conducted in practice. Data were gathered through non-participant observation, an analysis of minutes of governors' meetings, LEA documents and a questionnaire which also acted as an interview schedule. The report concludes that there is scope for developing the partnership between the school and the governing body in relation to the curriculum and proposes ways in which this might be approached.

Presentation

It is desirable, though not always essential for small-scale studies, that reports should be typed (check institutional rules). Typed copy should be in double spacing, with quotations (other than very short ones) indented and in single spacing. Pages should be numbered. Type or write on one side of the page only, leaving a left-hand margin of one and a half inches. Incidentally, whether you are sending your report to be typed or are submitting a handwritten copy, make sure your writing is legible. It is not fair to a typist, and it is not wise to annoy the examiner by handing in an illegible scrawl. Do not expect the typist to interpret your abbreviations or to make corrections. It is your job to hand in good copy.

The Need for Revision

Barzun and Graff (1977:31) remind us that 'NO ONE, HOWEVER GIFTED, CAN PRODUCE A PASSABLE FIRST DRAFT. WRITING MEANS REWRITING.' You may find you need two, three or even more drafts before you are satisfied with the final result, so time must be set aside for this writing and refining process.

One problem about spending so much time on the original draft (the most difficult part of the writing stage) is that parts of it may seem right simply because they have been read so often. Another is that you may be so familiar with the subject that you assume something is understandable to the reader when it is not. Time will give you a better perspective on your writing, so you should put the script aside — for several days if you can — so that you can return it with a more critical eye. This will help you to identify repetitive passages, errors of expression and lack of clarity

Work through your first draft section by section to ensure its sense, accuracy, logical sequencing and soundness of expression. (If you wrote only one paragraph on one side of each sheet, as suggested, this correcting and reordering stage will be relatively straightforward). In particular, check spelling, (always have a dictionary to hand), quotations, punctuation, referencing, the overuse of certain terms (a *Roget's Thesaurus* can help you to find alternative forms of expression), and grammar (particularly consistency of tense).

Remind yourself as you read that whatever structure has been selected, your readers will wish to be quite clear why you carried out the investigation, how you conducted it, what methods you used to gather your evidence and what you found out. It is not enough to describe; you will be expected to analyse, to evaluate and if the evidence merits it, to make recommendations.

If research findings are to be put into practice, they have to be presented in a way in which practitioners and policy-makers can understand them. Please bear this in mind when you present your projects. There is no special academic language that should be used in academic papers. Good, clear English remains good, clear English, whatever the context. Technical language may well save time when you are talking to colleagues with a similar background to your own, but it rarely translates well on to paper, and your readers (and your examiner) may become irritated by too much jargon or obscure language.

The need for revision and rewriting was emphasized in a recent radio interview, when a world-famous economist who had many scholarly books to his credit, was complimented by the interviewer on his style of writing. 'It must be a great advantage to you', said the interviewer, 'to be able to write so freely and so easily. How do you do it?' The economist revealed his secret as follows:

> First I produce a draft and then I leave it alone for a day or two. Then I go back to it and decide that it has been written by an ignoramus, so I throw it away. Then I produce a second draft and leave it alone for a few days. I read it and decide there are the germs of a few good ideas there, but it is so badly written that it is not worth keeping, so I throw it away. After a few days, I write the third draft. I leave it alone for a while and when I read it again I discover that the ideas are developing, that there is some coherence to my arguments and that the grammar is not too bad. I correct this draft, change paragraphs around, insert new thoughts, remove overlapping passages and begin to feel quite pleased with myself. After a few days, I read through this fourth draft, make final corrections and hand over the fifth draft to the typist. At that stage, I find I have usually achieved the degree of spontaneity for which I have been striving.

You may not need five drafts. Three may be enough if you write easily, but rest assured that no one gets away with one or two — and most of us take four or five.

When you have completed the writing to the best of your ability, try to enlist the help of someone who will read over the manuscript to look for remaining errors. Failing that, you could read your report out loud, though make sure you are alone or your family may feel the strain has been too much for you! Reading aloud is particularly useful for detecting the need for better linking passages.

Depending on what 'house' rules require, either write out a fair copy or give the final draft to the typist. If the report is to be typed, give clear instructions about layout, punctuation, headings and so on. It is your job to hand in good copy and to make it quite clear what is to be done. Check the final, typed copy. Even expert typists can make mistakes, and if your writing is bad, it is inevitable that mistakes will be made. Finally, congratulate yourself on an excellent job completed on time. Hand in the report and give yourself an evening off!

Writing the Report: General Checklist

1. Set deadlines.   Allocate dates for sections, sub-sections and the whole report. Keep an eye on your schedule.

2. Write regularly.

3. Create a rhythm of work.   Don't stop to check references. Make a note of what has to be checked, but don't stop.

4. Write up a section as soon as it is ready.

Try particularly to produce a draft of the literature review as soon as the bulk of your reading is completed.

5. Stop at a point from which it is easy to resume writing.

6. Leave space for revisions.

Use one side of the page only. Try to keep to one paragraph per page.

7. Publicize your plans.

You may need a little help from your friends to meet the deadlines.

8. Check that all essential sections have been covered.

Outline of the research, review of previous work, statement of the scope and aims of the investigation, description of procedures, statement of results, discussion, summary and conclusions, references, abstract.

9. Check length is according to institutional requirements.

You don't want to be failed on a technicality.

10. Don't forget the title page.

11. Any acknowledgements and thanks?

12. Include headings where possible.

Anything to make it easier for readers to follow the structure will help.

13. Number tables and figures and provide titles.

Check tables and figures for accuracy, particularly after typing.

14. Make sure all quotations are acknowledged.

Check that quotations are presented in a consistent format.

15. Provide a list of references.

Unless instructed otherwise, include only items to which reference is made in the report. Check that a consistent system is used and that there are no omissions.

16. Appendices should only include items that are required for reference purposes. Do not clutter the report with irrelevant items.

Unless instructed otherwise, one copy of each data-collecting instrument should be included.

17. Remember to leave sufficient time for revision and rewriting.

Check that you have written in plain English. Check that your writing is legible.

18. Try to get someone to read the report.	Fresh eyes will often see errors you have overlooked.

Writing the Report: Checklist before Handing Over to the Typist

If you were writing a critique of a piece of research done by someone else, you might ask the following questions. Before handing over what you hope will be your final draft for typing, subject your own report to the same sort of examination. Ask yourself:

1. Is the meaning clear? Are there any obscure passages?
2. Is the report well written? Check tenses, grammar, spelling, overlapping passages, punctuation, jargon.
3. Is the referencing well done? Are there any omissions?
4. Does the abstract give the reader a clear idea of what is in the report?
5. Does the title indicate the nature of the study?
6. Are the objectives of the study stated clearly?
7. Are the objectives fulfilled?
8. If hypotheses were postulated, were they testable? Are they proved or not proved?
9. Has a sufficient amount of literature relating to the topic been studied?
10. Does the literature review, if any, provide an indication of the state of knowledge in the subject? Is your topic placed in the context of the area of study as a whole?
11. Are all terms clearly defined?
12. Are the selected methods of data collection accurately described? Are they suitable for the task? Why were they chosen?
13. Are any limitations of the study clearly presented?
14. Have any statistical techniques been used? If so, are they appropriate for the task?
15. Are the data analysed and interpreted or merely described?
16. Are the results clearly presented? Are tables, diagrams and figures well drawn?
17. Are conclusions based on evidence? Have any claims been made that cannot be substantiated?
18. Is there any evidence of bias? Any emotive terms or intemperate language?
19. Are the data likely to be reliable? Could another researcher repeat the methods used and have a reasonable chance of getting the same or similar results?
20. Are recommendations (if any) feasible?
21. Are there any unnecessary items in the appendix?
22. Would you give the report a passing grade if you were the examiner? If not, perhaps an overhaul is necessary.

Postscript

There may be occasions when, in spite of careful planning and preparation, a project does not go according to plan. You may find that people who said they were willing to provide information by a certain date fail to do so, for example, or that results were not forthcoming. If things do go wrong, consult your tutor to discuss the best course of action. You may have learnt a great deal about conducting an investigation and the topic you were investigating, even though the outcome may not be what you had hoped. If you are not able to produce a report on the lines you planned, you may be able to submit a report of what you have been able to do, together with an account of what went wrong and why and, if appropriate, how you would have planned and carried out the investigation if you were starting again. The important thing is to ask for help. Intelligent people who are first-time researchers sometimes feel they ought to be able to sort themselves out, and by not making use of supervisors, computer-centre staff and librarians, may waste a great deal of time. I said in the Introduction to this book that we all learn how to do research by actually doing it. That is quite true, but anyone carrying out an investigation for the first time needs some assistance. Make sure you take advantage of any that is available.

Just one final word. People who agree to be interviewed or to complete questionnaires, diary forms or checklists, groups who agree to your observing meetings, and keepers of archives who allow you to consult documents, deserve consideration and thanks. Daphne Johnson sums up the position well:

> If files are left in disarray, papers borrowed and not returned, or respondents subjected to too lengthy or frequent interviews, at inconvenient times, the researcher's welcome will be worn out. All social researchers are to some extent mendicants, since they are seeking a free gift of time or information from those who are the subject of study. But researchers who bear this fact in mind, and who, without becoming the captive of their respondents, can contrive to make the research experience a helpful and profitable one, will almost certainly be gratified by the generosity with which people will give their time and knowledge.
>
> (Johnson 1984:11)

References

Adelman, C., Jenkins, D. and Kemmis, S. (1977). 'Re-thinking case study: notes from the second Cambridge conference', *Cambridge Journal of Education*, 6, 139–50.

Bales, R.F. (1950). *Interaction Process Analysis: A Method for the Study of Small Groups.* Cambridge, Mass., Addison-Wesley.

Barnett, V.D. and Lewis, T. (1963). 'A study of the relation between GCE and degree results', *Journal of the Royal Statistical Society*, A(126), 187–226.

Barnett, V.D., Holder, R.L. and Lewis, T. (1968). 'Some new results on the association between students' ages and their degree results', *Journal of the Royal Statistical Society*, A(131).

Bartholomew, J. (1971). 'The teacher as researcher', *Hard Cheese*, 1.

Barzun, J. and Graff, H.E. (1977). *The Modern Researcher.* 3rd edn, New York, Harcourt Brace Jovanovich.

Bassey, M. (1981). 'Pedagogic research: on the relative merits of search for generalization and study of single events', *Oxford Review of Education*, 7(1), 73–93.

Best, J.W. (1970). *Research in Education.* 2nd edn, New Jersey, Prentice-Hall.

Bogdan, R.C. and Biklen, S.K. (1982). *Qualitative Research for Education: An Introduction to Theory and Methods.* Boston, Mass., Allyn & Bacon.

Borg, W.R. (1981). *Applying Educational Research: A Practical Guide for Teachers.* New York, Longman.

Bradley, H.W. and Eggleston, J.F. (1976). *An Induction Year Experiment.* Report of an experiment carried out by Derbyshire, Lincolnshire and Nottinghamshire LEAs and the University of Nottingham School of Education. Nottingham University School of Education.

Bradley, J. and Silverleaf, J. (1979). *Making the Grade.* Windsor, NFER.

British Education Index (1954 on) (quarterly). London, British Library Bibliographic Services Division.

British Education Theses Index 1950–80 (1980). Leicester, Librarians of Institutes and Schools of Education.

British National Bibliography (1950 on) (weekly). London, British Library Bibliographic Services Division.

British Standards Institution (1970). *Abbreviation of Titles of Periodicals, Part 1, Principles* (BS 4148). London, British Standards Institution.

British Standards Institution (1978). *Citing Publications by Bibliographical References* (BS 5605). London, British Standards Institution.

Brown, F.L., Amos, J.R. and Mink, O.G. (1975). *Statistical Concepts: A Basic Programme*. 2nd edn, New York, Harper & Row.

Brown, Sally and McIntyre, Donald (1981). 'An action-research approach to innovation in centralized educational systems', *Eur. J. Sci. Educ.*, 3(3), 243–58.

Burgess, R.G. (1981). 'Keeping a research diary', *Cambridge Journal of Education*, 11, pt 1, 75–83.

Cohen, L. (1976). *Educational Research in Classrooms and Schools: A Manual of Materials and Methods*. London, Harper & Row.

Cohen, L. and Manion, L. (1980). *Research Methods in Education*. London, Croom Helm.

Cope, Edith and Gray, John (1979). 'Teachers as researchers: some experience of an alternative paradigm', *British Educational Research Journal*, 5(2), 237–251.

Dale, Sheila and Carty, Joan (1985). *Finding Out about Continuing Education*. Milton Keynes, Open University Press.

Derbyshire Education Committee (1966). 'Awards to students' (mimeo).

Drew, Clifford J. (1980), *Introduction to Designing and Conducting Research*. 2nd edn, Missouri, C.B. Mosby Company.

Eaton, E.G. (1980). 'The academic performance of mature age students: a review of the general literature', in T. Hore and L.H.T. West (eds.), *Mature Age Students in Australian Higher Education*, Higher Education Advisory and Research Unit, Monash University, Australia.

Eggleston, J. (1979). 'The characteristics of educational research: mapping the domain', *British Educational Research Journal* 5(1), 1–12.

Elliott, J., Bridges, D., Ebbutt, D., Gibson, R. and Nias, J. (1980) *School Accountability: The SSRC Cambridge Accountability Project*. London, Grant McIntyre.

Elton, G.R. (1967). *The Practice of History*. London, Fontana Library.

Fagin, M.C. (1971). *Life Experience Has Academic Value*. ERIC Document Reproduction Service, EDO47219.

Flanders, N.A. (1970). *Analysing Teaching Behaviour*, Cambridge, Mass., Addison-Wesley.

Flanagan, J.C. (1951). 'Defining the requirements of the executive's job', *Personnel*, 28, 28–35.

Flanagan, J.C. (1954). 'The critical incident technique', *Psychological Bulletin*, 51, 327–58.

Flecker, R. (1959). 'Characteristics of passing and failing students in first-year university mathematics', *The Educand* 3(3).

Fleming, W.G. (1959). *Personal and Academic Factors as Predictors of First Year Success in Ontario Universities*. Atkinson Study Report No. 5, University of Toronto, Department of Educational Research.

Forster, M. (1959). *An Audit of Academic Performance*.

Galton, M. (1978). *British Mirrors*. Leicester, University of Leicester School of Education.

Gavron, H. (1966). *The Captive Wife*. London, Routledge & Kegan Paul.

Grebenik, E. and Moser, C.A. (1962). 'Society: problems and methods of study', in A.T. Welford, M. Argyle, O. Glass and J.N. Morris (eds.), *Statistical Surveys*, London, Routledge & Kegan Paul.

Harris, D. (1940). 'Factors affecting college grades: a review of the literature', *Psychology Bulletin*, 37.

Haywood, P. and Wragg, E.C. (1982). *Evaluating the Literature*. Rediguide 2, University of Nottingham School of Education.

Hilsum, S. and Cane, B. (1971). *The Teacher's Day*. Windsor, NFER.

Hopkins, David (1985). *A Teacher's Guide to Classroom Research*. Milton Keynes, Open University Press.

Howard, K. and Sharp, J.A. (1983). *The Management of a Student Research Project*. Aldershot, Gower.

Howell, D.A. (1962). *A Study of the 1955 Entry to British Universities*. Evidence to the Robbins Committee on Higher Education. University of London (mimeo).

Johnson, D. (1984). 'Planning small-scale research', in Judith Bell, Tony Bush, Alan Fox, Jane Goodey and Sandy Goulding (eds.), *Conducting Small-Scale Investigations in Educational Management*. London, Harper & Row.

Kapur, K.L. (1972). 'Student wastage at Edinburgh University: factors related to failure and drop-out', *Universities Quarterly*, Summer.

Kitson Clark, G. (1967). *The Critical Historian*. London, Heinemann.

Kogan, M. (ed.) (1984). *School Governing Bodies*. London, Heinemann.

Krippendorf, K. (1980). *Content Analysis*. London, Sage.

Lacey, C. (1976). 'Problems of sociological fieldwork: a review of the methodology of "Hightown Grammar"', in M. Shipman (ed.), *The Organisation and Impact of Social Research*, London, Routledge & Kegan Paul.

Langeveld, M.J. (1965). 'In search of research', in *Paedagogica Europoea: The European Year Book of Educational Research*, Vol. 1. Amsterdam, Elsevier.

Lehmann, Irvin J. and Mehrens, William A. (1971). *Educational Research*. New York, Holt, Rinehart & Winston.

McCracken, D. (1969). *University Student Performance*. Report of the Student Health Department, University of Leeds.

Malleson, N.B. (1959). 'University student, 1953', I-Profile, *Universities Quarterly*, 13, 287–98.

Marples, D.L. (1967). 'Studies of managers: a fresh start', *Journal of Management Studies*, 4, 282–99.

Marwick, Arthur (1970). *The Nature of History*. London, Macmillan.

Marwick. Arthur (1977). *Introduction to History*. Units 3, 4 and 5 of A101, the Arts Foundation Course of the Open University. Milton Keynes, Open University Press.

Mayntz, R., Holm, K. and Hoebner, P. (1976). *Introduction to Empirical Sociology*. Harmondsworth, Penguin.

Minium, E.W. (1978). *Statistical Reasoning in Psychology and Education*. 2nd edn, New York, John Wiley.

Moser, C.A. and Kalton, G. (1971). *Survey Methods in Social Investigation*. 2nd edn, London, Heinemann.

Mountford, Sir J. (1957). *How They Fared: A Survey of a Three-year Student Entry.* Liverpool, Liverpool University Press.

Nie, H.N., Hull, C.H., Jenkins, J.G., Steinbrenner, K. and Brent, O.H. (1975). *Statistical Package for the Social Sciences (SPSS).* 2nd edn, New York, Holt, Rinehart & Winston.

Nisbet, J.D. (1977). 'Small-scale research: guidelines and suggestions for development', *Scottish Educational Studies,* 9, May, 13–17.

Nisbet, J.D. and Entwistle, N.J. (1970). *Educational Research Methods.* London, University of London Press.

Nisbet, J.D. and Watt, J. (1980). *Case Study.* Rediguide 26, University of Nottingham School of Education.

North, R.C., Holsti, O.R., Zaninovich, M.G. and Zinnes, D.A. (1963). *Content Analysis.* Evanston, Northwestern University Press.

Oppenheim, A.N. (1966). *Questionnaire Design and Attitude Measurement.* London, Heinemann.

Oxtoby, R. (1979). 'Problems facing heads of department', *Journal of Further and Higher Education.* 3(1), Spring, 46–59.

Peeke, G. (1984). 'Teacher as researcher', *Educational Research,* 26(1), February, 24–26.

Philips, H. and Cullen, A. (1955). 'Age and academic success', *Forum of Education,* 14.

Platt, J. (1981). 'On interviewing one's peers', *British Journal of Sociology,* 32(1), March, 75–91.

Preedy, M. and Riches, C. (1985). 'A methodological analysis of some research reports by practitioners on teacher–parent communications, for the Open University course Applied Studies in Educational Management (EP851)', School of Education, Open University (paper presented to BEMAS Conference 'Research and Administration in Secondary Education', Nov. 1985).

Raj, D. (1972) *The Design of Sample Surveys.* New York, McGraw-Hill.

Raven, Michael and Parker, Frank (1981). 'Research in education and the in-service student', *British Journal of In-Service Education,* 8(1), Autumn, 42–44.

Research into Higher Education Abstracts (1966 on) (3 per year). Abingdon, Carfax Publishing Co. on behalf of the Society for Research into Higher Education.

Richardson, Elizabeth (1973). *The Teacher, the School and the Task of Management.* London, Heinemann.

Robson, C. (1984) *Experiment, Design and Statistics in Psychology.* 2nd edn, Harmondsworth, Penguin.

Roget's Thesaurus of English Words and Phrases. 1982 edn, prepared by Susan M. Lloyd. Harlow, Longman.

Sanders, C. (1961). *Psychological and Educational Bases of Academic Performance.* Brisbane, Australian Council for Educational Research.

Sanders, C. (1963). 'Australian universities and their educational problems', *The Australian University,* 1, 2.

Sapsford, R.J. and Evans, J. (1984). 'Evaluating a research report', in Judith Bell, Tony Bush, Alan Fox, Jane Goodey and Sandy Goulding (eds.), *Conducting Small-Scale Investigations in Educational Management*. London, Harper & Row. Adapted from material prepared for Open University course DE304, *Research Methods in Education and the Social Sciences* (1979), Block 8, Part I, pp. 9–22.

School Organisation and Management Abstracts (1982 on) (quarterly). Abingdon, Carfax Publishing Co.

Scott, Christopher (1961). 'Research on Mail Surveys', *Journal of the Royal Statistical Society*, Series A, (124), 143–205.

Selkirk, K.E. (1980). *Sampling*. Rediguide 4. University of Nottingham School of Education.

Selltiz, C., Jahoda, M., Deutsch, M. and Cook, S.W. (1962) (2nd edition). *Research Methods in Social Relations*. New York, Holt, Rinehart & Winston, 1962.

Sharon, A.T. (1971). 'Adult academic achievement in relation to formal education and age', *Adult Education Journal*, 21.

Shaw, K.E. (1975). 'Negotiating curriculum change in a college of education', in W.A. Reid and D.F. Walker (eds.), *Case Studies in Curriculum Change*, London, Routledge & Kegan Paul.

Shaw, K.E. (1978). *Researching an Organisation*. Rediguide 24. University of Nottingham School of Education.

Simon, A. and Boyer, E. (1975). *The Reflective Practitioner*. New York, Basic Books.

Simons, H. (1984). 'Ethical principles in school self-evaluation', in Judith Bell, Tony Bush, Alan Fox, Jane Goodey and Sandy Goulding (eds.), *Conducting Small-Scale Investigations in Educational Management*, London, Harper & Row.

Small, J.J. (1966). *Achievement and Adjustment in the First Year at University*. Wellington, New Zealand Council for Educational Research.

Sociology of Education Abstracts (1965 on) (quarterly). Abingdon, Carfax Publishing Co.

Stuart, A. (1962). *Basic Ideas of Sampling*. London, Griffin.

Thomas, W., Beeby, C.E. and Oram, M.H. (1939). *Entrance to the University*. Wellington, New Zealand Council for Educational Research.

Travers, Robert M.W. (1958) *An Introduction to Educational Research*. 2nd edn, New York, Macmillan, 1964.

Turney, Billy and Robb, George (1971). *Research in Education: An Introduction*. Hinsdale, Ill. Dryden Press.

Ulrich's International Periodicals Directory (1983). *A classified guide to current periodicals, foreign and domestic*. Vol. 2, N–Z with indexes. 22nd edn. New York, R.R. Bowker Company.

Verma, G.K. and Beard, R.M. (1981). *What Is Educational Research? Perspectives on Techniques of Research*. Aldershot, Gower.

Vyas, H. (1979). 'The teacher as researcher', *Educational Review*, 11(3), Summer, 58–64.

Walker, P. (1975). 'The university performance of mature students', *Research in Education*, 14, 1–13.

Williams, G.L. (1984). 'Observing and Recording Meetings', in Judith Bell, Tony Bush, Alan Fox, Jane Goodey and Sandy Goulding (eds.), *Conducting Small-Scale Investigations in Educational Management*. London, Harper & Row.

Wilson, N.J. (1979). 'The ethnographic style of research', in Block 1 (*Variety in Social Science Research*), Part I (*Styles of Research*) of Open University course DE304, *Research Methods in Education and the Social Sciences*.

Wiseman, J.P. and Aron, M.S. (1972). *Field Reports in Sociology*. London, Transworld Publishers.

Woodley, A. (1979). 'The Prediction of Degree Performance among Undergraduates in the Commerce and Social Science Faculty', University of Birmingham, (unpublished).

Woodley, A. (1985). 'Taking account of mature students', in David Jaques and John Richardson (eds.), *The Future of Higher Education*. Guildford, SRHE and NFER-Nelson.

Wragg, E.C. (1980). *Conducting and Analysing Interviews*. Rediguide 11. University of Nottingham School of Education.

Wragg, E.C. and Kerry, T.L. (1978). *Classroom Interaction Research*. Rediguide 14. University of Nottingham School of Education.

Youngman, M.B. (1978). *Statistical Strategies*. Rediguide 20. University of Nottingham School of Education.

Youngman, M.B. (1979). *Analysing Social and Educational Research Data*. Maidenhead, McGraw-Hill.

Youngman, M.B. (1984). *Foundation Statistics for Education: Part I Principles* (January). *Part II Procedures* (March). University of Nottingham School of Education.

Youngman, M.B. (1986). *Analysing Questionnaires*. University of Nottingham School of Education.

Zimmerman, D.H. and Wieder, D.L. (1977). 'The diary-interview method', *Urban Life*, 5(4), January, 479–499.

Index